D0843274

Currency Substitution

Currency Substitution

Theory and Evidence from Latin America

Victor A. Canto
A.B. Laffer and Associates

Gerald Nickelsburg
University of Southern California

Kluwer Academic Publishers
Boston/Dordrecht/Lancaster

Distributors

for North America: Kluwer Academic Publishers, 101 Philip
Drive, Assinippi Park, Norwell, MA 02061, USA

for the UK and Ireland: Kluwer Academic Publishers, MTP Press
Limited, Falcon House, Queen Square, Lancaster LA1 1RN, UK

for all other countries: Kluwer Academic Publishers Group,
Distribution Centre, Post Office Box 322, 3300 AH Dordrecht, The
Netherlands

Library of Congress Cataloging-in-Publication Data

Canto, Victor A.
  Currency substitution.

  Bibliography: p.
  Includes index.
  1. Foreign exchange-Mathematical models.
  2. Equilibrium (Economics)-Mathematical models.
  3. Substitution (Economics)-Mathematical models.
  4. Currency question-Latin America-Mathematical models.
  5. Money supply-Latin America-Mathematical models.
  6. Monetary policy-Latin America-Mathematical models. 7. Inflation (Finance)-Latin America-Mathematical models. I.
  Nickelsburg, Gerald.
  II. Title.
  HG3823.C36 1987   332.4'56'098   86-27747
  ISBN 0-89838-195-9

Printed in the United States of America

TABLE OF CONTENTS

CONTENTS (CONT'D)

PREFACE

This work grew out of a series of investigations begun by the authors in 1980 and 1981. Specifically the authors pursued two lines of inquiry. First, to advance the state of the theoretical literature to better explain the crises of liberalization which seemed to be afflicting the third world in general and Latin America in particular. To do this, several different kinds of models were investigated and adapted. These are presented in Chapters 2, 3 and 5. Secondly an analysis of the empirical evidence was conducted in order to gain insight into the processes that were thought to be occurring and the theoretical models that were being developed. Some of this work appears in Chapters 3, 4, 5 and 6. Other work by the authors on these issues has been published elsewhere and is referenced herein.

There are a great many people whose work and whose comments have influenced this work. We would like to especially thank Guillermo Calvo, Michael Connolly, Sebastian Edwards, Roque Fernandez, Michael Darby, Robert Clower, Neil Wallace, John Kareken, Paul McNelis, Jeffrey Nugent, Jaime Marquez, Lee Ohanian, Leroy Laney, Jorge Braga de Macedo, Dale Henderson,

Matthew Canzoneiri, Arthur Laffer, Marc Miles, and George Von Furstenberg whose ideas and comments gave rise to much of our work. We would like to thank Suh Lee for his assistance with the computations in Chapter 5. We especially would like to thank Sharon Koga whose long hours of diligent typing and proofreading made the timely completion of this work possible.

Currency Substitution

CHAPTER 1

Introduction

The Latin American monetary experience over the last several decades has posed a multitude of questions for traditional monetary theory. First, the basic propositions of the relationship between the quantity of money, the rate of inflation and the rate of exchange depreciation do not seem, at least at a superficial level, to hold (see Vogel (1974)). Secondly, stabilization policy seems to result in increased rather than decreased inflation in many cases (see Sjaastad (1983) and Calvo (1983)). Third, with very high rates of inflation and very large negative real interest rates on domestic currency and nominally denominated domestic assets, the local currency is still being used (see Nickelsburg (1986b), Canto (1985)). Fourth, the velocity of money appears to be much more volatile than previously thought (McNelis and Nickelsburg (1986)). In this book we attempt to address these issues by reformulating monetary theory for a set of economies which have particularly tenuous monetary equilibria, tenuous because of their size, involvement in international trade and political credibility, and apply this theory to the experiences of four countries in Latin America; The Dominican Republic, Argentina, Venezuela and Ecuador. Although there is much research to be done in this area, our approach proves to be promising because we are able to develop a theoretical structure consistent with individual rationality which provides a reasonable explanation for many anomolous monetary phenomena related to stabilization and liberalization policy.

Our starting point is the theory of currency substitution. This area has been examined carefully by many researchers. The pioneering theoretical research was done by Calvo and Rodriguez (1977), Girton and Roper (1981) and Miles (1978). This research showed that it is possible for equilibria to be defined such that the level of foreign money in the domestic economy could play an important role, and that instability might possibly occur. The issue of instability in the Calvo and Rodriguez model was addressed by appealing to the rational expectations argument of Sargent and Wallace (1973) that the unstable paths are inconsistent with rational behavior. Canto and Nickelsburg (1983) showed how the Calvo and Rodriguez model could be altered to yield rational unstable paths.

A different but closely related line of theoretical research grew out of the idea that, as a modelling methodology, beginning with currencies as perfect substitutes was the appropriate first step. Kareken and Wallace (1981) analyzed the perfect substitute case in an overlapping generations framework and Helpman and Razin (1979) analyzed the same case using long lived agents. Both find that in the limit, currency substitution implies indeterminate exchange rates and prices, and that without some institutional framework differentiating the asset qualities of different fiat monies, there would be just one world money. This is consistent with the one world money approach of McKinnon (1982), Whitman (1975) and others. From these models Nickelsburg (1984) showed that perfect substitutability could be eliminated in a natural way by introducing uncertainty about policy regime change and capital controls, but that some of the serious policy implications from this approach remain.

The empirical research on currency substitution has yielded mixed results. Brittain (1981), Aktar and Putnam (1980), and Miles (1978) find evidence of currency substitution in developed economies, but Laney, Radcliffe and Willet (1984), Cuddington (1983), Bordo and Choudhri (1982) and others criticize their methodology. It is now generally agreed that while currency substitution in the sense of portfolio diversification may exist in the developed world, it is indistinguishable from highly integrated capital markets. Therefore the analysis of a separate cause of financial instability is neither warranted nor important.

Many researchers working on Latin America have noticed that the empirical monetary phenomena they observe are somewhat more sympathetic to the currency substitution approach. This evidence has been observed for the Dominican Republic by Canto (1985), Bolivia by Jameson (1985) and Melvin (1984), Ecuador by Nickelsburg (1986a, 1986b), Peru by McNelis and Nickelsburg (1986), Venezuela by Marquez (1985), Mexico by Melvin (1984), Ortiz (1983) and Laney (1981) and more generally by Tanzi and Blejer (1982) and Ohanian (1986). Their results indicate that further theoretical analysis, analysis that distinguishes between developed country monetary arrangements and Latin American or LDC monetary arrangements, is warranted.

The characteristics we believe differentiate the two sets of monetary arrangements revolve around two key aspects of any monetary system. First, if the type of money used within an economy is fiat money, then the demand for that money, its mean level as well as its variance, will depend crucially on the faith that the people of that country have in their money. This means that they will have to form expectations about the future course of the money stock and of prices. These expectations will pose questions about the certainty of particular monetary policies, the inertial power of the past observed relationships between key economic variables and the permanency of current legal market arrangements. In developed economies stable and predictable political systems and generally conservative economic policy in the sense of being slow to be changed radically imply that the expectations problem, although difficult, only involves forecasting future prices based on past economic policy and current policy pronouncements. In Latin America, we contend, the situation is quite different. Specifically, radical institutional changes are quite common. Political instability engenders such changes in response to crisis situations, situations which occur with unfortunate frequency. Therefore, policy pronouncements must be seriously evaluated as to the probability of follow-up implementations of them and the ability of the government to maintain them. Moreover, the probability of the current government remaining in power must be assessed. Finally, money issuance is a major source of revenue for many of these countries and a prediction of relatively stable inflation rates is bound to be wrong.

Secondly, tenuous monetary equilibria require alternative media of exchange. Money is demanded because it provides services to its users and these services are substantial. This is precisely why an otherwise unvalued item such as fiat money can coexist with safe stores of value such as government or blue-chip bonds. It is therefore very difficult to drive people to use something other than money as a medium of exchange, even during periods of high inflation. They may conserve on their use of money, but historical observation says that they will rarely abandon it.

In Latin America most countries are relatively open and are heavily involved in foreign trade. With a large part of GNP being created by foreign trade it is important for individuals to know something about the course of the world economy. Because of economies to scale, information on world economic performance for the general public and the marginal cost of additional information on the world economy is therefore cheaper than in the developed world. For many of these countries, the majority of their exports are sold in world markets for dollars. Thus, it is also important for individuals to have knowledge of the course of the dollar for business planning. Again, economies to scale in information gathering lower the cost of information about the U.S. dollar. Third, a heavy involvement in international trade makes available a large number of dollars for use as a substitute to the domestic currency. With these three properties of expatriate dollars; ready availability, low cost information about world economic performance and low cost information about the course of the dollar; U.S. dollars are a natural substitute for the domestic money.

That dollars and the domestic currency are not perfect substitutes stems from two important institution restraints. First, obtaining information about foreign economic policy may be inexpensive, but it must be more expensive than obtaining information about the domestic economy. Therefore, at equal inflation rates the steady state equilibrium will not have domestic residents hold foreign money. Secondly, because the money is foreign money the domestic government can impose restrictions on its use, restrictions which they would not impose on their own money. This happened, for example, when Mexico nationalized dollar deposits in Mexican banks in 1982.

We begin our analysis by modelling these aspects of an economic environment in a general equilibrium setting in Chapter 2. First, it is shown that the exchange rate is indeterminate, even in a stochastic setting, without some overlay of monetary institutions. We then derive the minimum requirements for those institutions and present some welfare results. These results indicate that intervention to prevent capital flight may be optimal under certain conditions especially in the presence of stabilization policy. Chapter 3 analyzes a simpler aggregate model which embodies our more general theory. This is done in an attempt to make our model more empirically tractable. We illustrate this concept with some casual evidence from the Dominican Republic. Chapter 4 carries the empirical work further by analyzing a structural model of the Dominican Republic. Chapter 5 presents an analysis of an inflation ridden — sometimes open economy, Argentina, to ascertain if it is consistent with our theory. Finally we compare the oil shock experiences of Venezuela and Ecuador.

The theory and the empirical work is very suggestive. In particular it suggests that governments need to be cognizant of the limitations of liberalization and stabilization policy when domestic residents have the option of choosing away from the domestic money. If they are not, they will force a capital flight which will drain the country of its wealth, and they will make it increasingly attractive for domestic residents to use foreign currency. If the latter occurs, not only will stabilization policy fail to work, but the ability to collect any seignorage from domestic money issuance will be severely impaired. These implications of the work we present here corresponds with the experiences of Latin American experiments with stabilization and liberalization policies.

REFERENCES

Aktar, M.A. and B.H. Putnam, 1980, Money demand and foreign exchange risk: the German case, 1972-1976, *Journal of Finance* 35, 787-793.

Bordo, M.D. and E. Choudhri, 1982, Currency substitution and the demand for money: some evidence for Canada, *Journal of Money Credit and Banking* 14, 47-57.

Brittain, B., 1981, International currency substitution and the apparent instability of velocity in some European economies and in the United States, *Journal of Money Credit and Banking* 13, 135-155.

Calvo, G.A., 1983, Lecciones del monetarismo: el cono sud, paper presented at the 37th anniversary of the Dominican Republic Central Bank.

Calvo, G.A. and C.A. Rodriguez, 1977, A model of exchange rate determination under currency substitution and rational expectations, *Journal of Political Economy* 85, 617-625.

Canto, V., 1985, Monetary policy, 'dollarization,' and parallel market exchange rates: the case of the Dominican Republic, *Journal of International Money and Finance* 4, 507-521.

Canto, V. and G. Nickelsburg, 1983, Towards a theory of currency choice and currency crisis in *Dynamic Modelling and Control of national Economies*, T. Basar and L.F. Pau, eds. Pergamon Press: New York, 371-378.

Girton, L. and D. Roper, 1981, The theory and implications of currency substitution, *Journal of Money Credit and Banking* 13, 12-30.

Helpman, E. and A. Razin, 1979, Towards a consistent comparison of alternative exchange rate systems, *Canadian Journal of Economics* 12, 394-409.

Jameson, K.P., 1985, Dollarization and de-dollarization in Bolivia, manuscript, Department of Economics, University of Notre Dame.

Kareken, J. and N. Wallace, 1981, On the indeterminacy of equi-
    librium exchange rates, *Quarterly Journal of Economics* 96,
    207-222.

Laney, L.O., 1981, Currency substitution: the Mexican case, *Voice
    of the Federal Reserve Bank of Dallas*, 1-10.

Laney, L.O. and C.D. Radcliffe and T.D. Willet, 1984, Interna-
    tional currency substitution by Americans is not high, *South-
    ern Economic Journal*, 1196-1203.

Marquez, J., 1985, Money demand in open economies: a currency
    substitution model for Venezuela, manuscript, International
    Finance Division, Board of Governors of the Federal Reserve
    System, Washington, D.C.

Melvin, M., 1984, The dollarization of Latin America: a market
    enforced monetary reform, manuscript, Arizona State Univer-
    sity.

Miles, M.A., 1978, Currency substitution, flexible exchange rates,
    and monetary independence, *American Economic Review* 68,
    428-436.

McKinnon, R.I., 1982, Currency substitution and instability in
    the world dollar standard, *American Economic Review* 72,
    320-333.

McNelis, P. and G. Nickelsburg, 1986, Money, prices and dollar-
    ization: evidence from Ecuador and Peru, manauscript, De-
    partment of Economics, University of Southern California.

Nickelsburg, G., 1984, Flexible exchange rates with uncertain gov-
    ernment policy, *Review of Economic Studies* 51, 501-519.

Nickelsburg, G., 1986a, Inflation, expectations and qualitative
    government policy: Ecuador 1970-1982, *World Development*,
    forthcoming.

Nickelsburg, G., 1986b, Rediscounting private dollar debt and cap-
    ital flight in Ecuador, *Journal of International Money and
    Finance*, forthcoming.

Ohanian, L., 1985, Currency substitution and prices in Latin America: what have we learned from the evidence?, manuscript, Department of Economics, Security Pacific Bank, Los Angeles, CA.

Ortiz, G., 1983, Currency substitution in Mexico, *Journal of Money Credit and Banking* 15, 173-185.

Sargent, T. and N. Wallace, 1973, The stability of models of money and growth with perfect foresight, *Econometrica* 41, 1043-1048.

Sjaastad, L., 1983, Failure of economic liberalization in the case of Latin America, *World Economic Affairs* 1, 5-26.

Tanzi, V. and M. Blejer, 1982, Inflation, interest rates and currency substitution in developing countries; a discussion of the major issues, *World Development*, 781-790.

Vogel, R., 1974, The dynamics of inflation in Latin American 1950-1969, *American Economic Review* 64, 102-114.

Whitman, M.V.N., 1975, Global monetarism and the monetary approach to the balance of payments, *Brookings Papers of Economic Activity* 3, 491-536.

CHAPTER 2

A General Equilibrium Theory of
Exchange Rates and Managed Floating

The notion of exchange rate equilibria which are unstable or are strongly expectationally dependent finds little support in the theoretical literature. This is surprising since casual observation suggests incorporating the idea of rapidly fluctuating exchange rates and prices is appropriate for modelling developing country monetary phenomena. Nevertheless, the incorporation of rapid fluctuations in exchange rates is quite difficult except as an unexplained exogenous variation since generally endogenously arising fluctuations give rise to exploitable profit opportunities. In this chapter we present, following Kareken and Wallace (1977, 1981), Helpman and Razin (1979) and Nickelsburg (1980, 1984) a general equilibrium framework for the analysis of exchange rate fluctuations. We begin with an analysis of the indeterminacy of foreign exchange rate equilibria in a stochastic model. The third section of this chapter discusses the resolution of the indeterminacy problem and the fourth section presents welfare results for the "dirty" of managed floating exchange rate regimes.

1. MULTIPLE STOCHASTIC EXCHANGE RATE EQUILIBRIA

In a recent contribution Kareken and Wallace (1981) prove that in a model of fiat monies the *laissez faire* exchange rate equilibrium is indeterminate. Moreover there exists an uncountable number of perfect foresight equilibria, each with a different equilibrium foreign exchange rate. They conclude their study with the comment: "at this point, all we can do is observe that if our conjecture (on the robust character of the result) is established, then economists will have to go back to the issue of which among the several possible is the best of international economic policy regime."

In this section we examine the question of robustness, and establish the existence of a multiplicity of exchange rate equilibria when the environment is stochastic. The extension of the Kareken-Wallace framework is accomplished by introducing one simple source of randomness and by imposing the restriction of rational expectations on model agents. A generalization of this example to many sources of randomness is seen to be straightforward and without substantive change in the Kareken-Wallace result. Therefore, the Kareken-Wallace indeterminacy, at least in this dimension, is seen to be robust.

As will be seen the structure of the model is somewhat stringent. However the results are derived from basic rationality and optimization principles. In any model in which two monies are competing without actual or implied legal restrictions, and in which the monies are truly fiat monies, one can expect the same results. What is perhaps surprising about the results here is that the existence of different relative sizes of money stocks in different uncertain future states of the world makes no difference whatsoever in the relative prices of monies. Thus the natural generalization to real assets with state specific rates of return, does not alter the result if both monies retain positive value. Therefore the Kareken-Wallace assertion that economists studying exchange rates should first focus on environmental aspects which differentiate monies as assets holds *a fortiori* here.

1.1 The Model.

The basic framework is the Samuelson overlapping-generations model, and the specific structure of the model differs from Kareken and Wallace only in a specification of the uncertain environment. The following definitions and assumptions constitute the model but will be altered somewhat in sections 2 and 3.

a.1 There exist two countries (without loss of generality) indexed by k. The population of each country is immobile, time independent and of size $2N_k$.

a.2 At the beginning of each time t, N_k agents are born in country k, and each agent lives for two periods, t and $t + 1$.

a.3 $M_k(t)$ is the aggregate country k money stock at t and $m_i^k(t)$ is the individual country k agent purchase of money i at t. Ω_t is the information set available to agents at t; $\mathcal{E}$ is the mathematical expectation operator; and $\mathcal{E}_t$ is $\mathcal{E}$ conditional on Ω_t.

a.4 There exists one non-storable good. Each agent is endowed at the beginning of life with y_k of the good and receives no other endowment of it. $C_i^k(t)$ is defined as the consumption of the good by a citizen of country k, at time t in period i of the agents life.

a.5 Each agent of generation $s \geq 1$ has the utility function U : $R_+^2 \to R_+$. U is separable, homothetic, twice differentiable and increasing in its arguments. U is written as:

$$U\big(C_1^k(t), C_2^k(t + 1)\big) = V_1\big(C_1^k(t)\big) + V_2\big(C_2^k(t + 1)\big).$$

Define $f : R_+^2 \to R_+$ by $f = V_1'/V_2'$. U is defined such that f has the properties: $f > 0$, $f' < 0$; $f \to +\infty$ as $\big(C_1^k(t)/C_2^k(t+1)\big) \to 0$ and $f \to 0$ as $\big(C_1^k(t)/C_2^k(t + 1)\big) \to +\infty$; $\gamma_k > \big(C_1^k(t)/C_2^k(t + 1)\big)f'/f \geq -1$, where γ is defined in the proof of the existence theorem, and f is uniformly continuous.

a.6 The N_k generation 0 agents of country k have the utility function $U : R_+ \to R_+$ defined as $U\big(C_2^k(1)\big) = V_2\big(C_2^k(1)\big)$, where V_2 is the same function as V_2 in 5.

a.7 Define the variate $X_k(t)$ by:

$$X_k(t) = 1 - \left(m_k^k(t) - a\right) N_k / M_k(t)$$

where a is a constant. Define $\tilde{Z} : R_+^2 \to R_{++}^2$ as a Baire function;

n and the triple (R_+^2, B, μ) where $\mu(\tilde{Z})$ is a probability measure on

the Borel sets B of R_+^2. $\tilde{Z}$ is then a measurable random variable

of dimension 2×1 on R_+^2; denote its elements $\tilde{Z}_k$. Define the

function $Z : R_+^2 \to R_+^2$ by:

$$Z_k(t) = \begin{cases} \tilde{Z}_k(t) & \text{if } \tilde{Z}_k(t) > X_k(t-1) \\ X_k(t-1) & \text{otherwise.} \end{cases}$$

The money stock growth rule is a random variable defined by:

$M_k(t+1) = Z_k(t) M_k(t)$.

a.8 Citizens of country k receive at the beginning of their second

period of life $(t+1)$ an endowment $x^k(t) = M_k(t)\left(Z_k(t) - 1\right)/N_k$

units of country k money.

a.9 Ω contains realized values of all variables and constants at

times $s \le t$ and the structure of the model. $P_k(t)$ is the commodity

price of money k at t, and $E(t)$ is the price of money 2 in units of

money 1.

a.10 Agents behave as competitive price takers, and there are no

restrictions on commodity or money exchange. Agents of age 1 at

t seek a maximum of $\mathcal{E}_t U$ and agents of age 2 at t seek a maximum of $\mathcal{E}_t V_2$ subject to the constraints:

$$C_1^k(t) + \Sigma_i P_i(t) m_i^k(t) \leq y_k$$

$$C_2^k(t) \leq \Sigma_i P_i(t) m_i^k(t-1) | X^k(t-1) P_k(t)$$

by choosing $C_1^k(t)$, $C_2^k(t+1)$, $m_1^k(t)$, $M_2^k(t)$.

Before proceeding to the main result, a comment on the model assumptions is in order. The one assumption that is stronger than in Kareken and Wallace is the bound γ on the marginal rate of substitution function. Perhaps the natural interpretation of this is that the restriction implies a bound on the responsiveness of agents to changes in the rate of return on assets. (This interpretation is suggested in Bental (1979)). The gross substitutes condition requires some agent response, but the bound, in effect, says the response cannot be too great. This restriction is used to compactify the space of possible equilibria, and it is a sufficient but not necessary assumption.

Secondly, the random variable Z_k was defined in an indirect way. The purpose of this was to insure the stationarity of the underlying random variable, while at the same time preventing government policy rules from possibly taxing away any agents entire real balance. Thus, the c.d.f. of the $\tilde{Z}$ vector defined as $G(\tilde{Z}^*) = \int_0^{\tilde{Z}^*} \mu(dZ)$ is time stationary, but $X_n(t)$ and therefore the random variable Z_k is not necessarily time stationary.

1.2 Multiple Equilibria.

This section presents a theorem establishing the existence of an uncountable number of equilibria for our model. To accomplish this we define $q_k(t) = P_1(t)m_1^k(t) + P_2(t)m_2^k(t)$ as the real balances chosen by an agent of country k at time t. Assumptions a.1, a.4, a.5 and a.6 permit the suppression of aggregation problems, and only a typical country k agent will be considered. An equilibrium is defined as a sequnece $\{q_1(t), q_2(t)\}$ varying over $t = 1, 2, \ldots$ such that the chosen sequence is a maximum in the sense of a.10 and a requirement of aggregate money stocks being freely held by agents and the aggregate good stock be entirely consumed by agents.

The candidate sequences will be chosen as bounded continuous and differentiable functions of the state of the economy. Let $\lambda(t) = M_1(t)/(M_1(t) + E(t)M_2(t))$. Then $\lambda(t + 1) = (Z_1(t + 1)/Z_2(t + 1))/((Z_1(t + 1)/Z_2(t + 1)) - 1 + \lambda(t)^{-1})$ which will be denoted by the stochastic difference equation; $\lambda(t + 1) = g(\lambda(t), Z_1(t + 1)/Z_2(t + 1))$. Since Z_k is bounded away from zero and $\lambda(t) \in (0, 1), g$ exists. The constancy of all other exogenous variables means $\eta(t)$ is a complete description of the time varying component of the state vector. The space $L_\infty[0, y_k]$ of bounded functions of λ is considered with norms $\|L(\lambda)\| = ess \ sup |L(\lambda)|$

for $L \in L_\infty[0, y_k]$. Define S_k as the complete subspace of $L_\infty[0, y_k]$ by: if $L \in S_k$ the L is continuous, everywhere differentiable and $\|L'(\lambda)\| \leq K$. Then candidate functions for $q_k(t)$ will be elements $L_k(\lambda)$ of S_k. Thus, an equilibrium of this kind will be time stationary in the sense of real balance decision rules being time stationary.

THEOREM 1: *Let:*

i) $\bar{E}, E^*$ *be arbitrary constants in the interval* $[0, +\infty)$;

ii) *Assumptions 1-10 hold;*

iii) $M_k(0) = \bar{M}, M_k(0)$ *distributed arbitrarily as* $m_k^i(0)$ *to agents of generation 0 at time* $t = 1$ $k, i = 1, 2.$

Then:

i) *For each* $\bar{E} \ni L_k(\lambda)$, $k = 1, 2$ *such that* $L_k \in S_k$ *and* $L_k(\lambda(t)) = q_k(t)$ *satisfies assumption 10.*

$$\Sigma_k N_k m_i^k(t) = M_i(t) \quad i = 1, 2$$

$$\Sigma_k N_k C_1^k(t) + \Sigma_k N_k C_2^k(t) = \Sigma_k N_k y_k$$

ii) $|q_k(t, E) - q_k(t, E^*)| \neq 0$ *for* $\bar{E} \neq E^*.$

The proof of the theorem is somewhat involved and is reserved for Section 1.3. The essential idea of the proof is to show that the satisfaction of assumption 10 is equivalent to a continuous mapping of the space S_k into itself, and then to prove existence by invoking the Schauder fixed point theorem.

The above theorem illustrates the generality of Kareken and Wallace's indeterminacy result with respect to a stochastic environment. It is clear that stochastic endowments or even stochastic utility functions from the class considered here will not alter this result. Moreover, the presence of additional assets will not substantially alter the result. Assets with given or random returns may force one money out of use; but so long as both monies are being used, they must compete against each other, and it is this which engenders the result.

1.3 Mathematical Appendix

Proof of Theorem 1

The first step of the proof is to algebraically manipulate the optimal real balances as defined in assumption a.10. Let $Q(t) = P_1(t)M_1(t) + P_2(t)M_2(t)$. Then the constrained optimal q_k satisfy

$$
\begin{aligned}
q_k(t) = \int_{\tilde{Z}} f_k q_k(t) \left((Z_1/Z_2) - 1 + \lambda(t)^{-1} \right)^{-1} \\
\times \lambda(t)^{-1} Q(t)^{-1} Q(t+1) \mu(d\tilde{Z}),
\end{aligned}
\tag{2.1.1}
$$

where;

$$f_k \equiv V_2'\Big(Q(t+1)\big((Z_1/Z_2) - 1 + \lambda(t)^{-1}\big)^{-1}$$
$$\times Z_2^{-1}\big(\lambda(t)^{-1}Q(t)^{-1}q_k(t) \qquad (2.1.2)$$
$$+ N_k^{-1}(Z_k - 1)n_k\big)\big)/V_1'\big(y_k - q_k(t)\big)$$

$$n_1 = 1 \text{ and } n_2 = \lambda(t)^{-1}\big(1 - \lambda(t)\big).$$

Condition (2.1.1) will be employed to determine an optimal real balance decision rule. The second step of the proof is to define the mapping. Let $L_k \in S_k$ and $L_3 = N_1 L_1 + N_2 L_2$. a.1 is then written as the mapping $\phi : S_k \times \Sigma_k \to S \times S$ by:

$$\begin{bmatrix} L_1^*\big(\lambda(t)\big) \\ L_2^*\big(\lambda(t)\big) \end{bmatrix} = \phi \begin{bmatrix} L_1\big(\lambda(t)\big) \\ L_2\big(\lambda(t)\big) \end{bmatrix}. \qquad (2.1.3)$$

A fixed point of ϕ will be optimal decision vector in $S_k \times S_k$.

To show ϕ preserves continuity consider the sequence $\{L_1^n(\lambda), L_2^n(\lambda)\}$ such that $\lim \|(L_1(\lambda), L_2(\lambda)) - (L_1^n(\lambda), L_2^n(\lambda))\| = 0$ as $n \to \infty$. By the uniform continuity of g, f_k, L_3; $\forall \in > 0 \exists N$, such that $\forall n > N$, $k = 1,2$; $\|f_k(L_1(\lambda), L_2(\lambda))L_k(\lambda)L_3(\lambda) \times L_3(g(\lambda, Z_1/Z_2)) - f_k(L_1^n(\lambda), L_2^n(\lambda))L_k^n(\lambda)L_3^n(\lambda)L_3^n(g(\lambda, Z_1/Z_2))\| < \epsilon$, then: $\|\phi(L_1(\lambda), L_2(\lambda)) - \phi(L_1^n(\lambda), L_2^n(\lambda))\| = \Big\| \Big[\int_{\tilde{Z}} \Big(f_k(L_1(\lambda), L_2(\lambda))L_k(\lambda)L_3(\lambda)L_3(g(\lambda, Z_1/Z_2)) - f_k(L_1^n(\lambda), L_2^n \times (\lambda))L_k^h(\lambda)L_3^h(g(\lambda, Z_1/Z_2))\Big)(Z_1/Z_2 - 1 + \lambda^{-1})Z_2^{-1}\lambda^{-1}\mu(d\tilde{Z})\Big]\Big\| \le$

$\epsilon \left\| \left[\int_{\tilde{Z}} (Z_1/Z_2 - 1 + \lambda^{-1}) Z_2^{-1} \lambda^{-1} \mu(d\tilde{Z}) \right] \right\| \ \forall \ n > N$. But, ϵ is arbitrary and the integral is finite. Therefore $\phi(L_1^n(\lambda), L_2^n(\lambda)) \to \phi(L_1(\lambda), L_2(\lambda))$ in $\|.\|$ as $n \to \infty$. (Note: the λ subscript is everywhere t.)

To show ϕ preserves bounded derivatives write the integrand of (2.1.1) as $\alpha_k(\lambda) f_k(\lambda)$; define $\bar{\gamma}_k(\lambda) = f'(C_1^k(t)/C_2^k(t))/f$ where f is defined as in a.5 and define $\gamma_3(\lambda) = ((Z_1/Z_2)\lambda + 1 - \lambda)^{-1}$. The time argument of Z_k is everywhere $t + 1$; the time argument of λ is everywhere t; and where there is no ambiguity arguments are suppressed.

The derivatives of α_k, f_k and $X_k(t) P_k(t + 1)$ are:

$$d\alpha_k/d\lambda = \left(Z_2^{-1} L_3(g) L_3(\lambda)^{-1} L_k(\lambda) \right) \bar{\gamma}_3'$$
$$+ \left(Z_2^{-1} \bar{\gamma}_3 L_3(\lambda)^{-1} L_3(g) \right) L_k'(\lambda)$$
$$+ \left(Z_2^{-1} \bar{\gamma}_3 L_3(\lambda)^{-1} L_k(\lambda) \right) \left(N_1 L_1'(g) + N_2 L_2'(g) \right)$$
$$- \left(Z_2^{-1} \bar{\gamma}_3 L_3(g) L_3(\lambda)^{-2} L_k(\lambda) \right) \left(N_1 L_1'(\lambda) + N_2 L_2'(\lambda) \right).$$
$$df_k/d\lambda = \left(f_k \bar{\gamma}_k (C_1^k)^{-1} \right) L_k'(\lambda)$$
$$+ f_k \bar{\gamma}_k (C_2^k)^{-1} \left(d\alpha_k/d\lambda + dP_k(t + 1) X_k(t)/d\lambda \right),$$

$$dP_k(t + 1) X_k(t)/d\lambda = \left(N_k^{-1} (Z_1/Z_2) \lambda n_k \bar{\gamma}_3 \right) \left(N_1 L_1'(g) + N_2 L_2'(g) \right)$$
$$+ \left(N_k^{-1} (Z_k^{-1}) (Z_1/Z_2) L_3(g) \right)$$
$$\times \left(\bar{\gamma}_3 (n_k + \lambda n_k') + \lambda n_k \bar{\gamma}_3' \right)$$

Substituting into the derivative of the integrand with respect to γ:

$$
\begin{aligned}
df_k\alpha_k/d\lambda &= \Big[f_k Z_2^{-1} L_3(g) \big[(\alpha_k \bar{\gamma}_k (C_2^k)^{-1} + 1)(L_3(\lambda)^{-1} L_k(\lambda)) \gamma_3' \\
&\quad + (\alpha_k \bar{\gamma}_k (C_2^k)^{-1})(N_k^{-1}(Z_k - 1)Z_1) \\
&\quad \times (\lambda n_k \gamma_3' + \gamma_3 n_k + \gamma_3 \lambda n_k') \big] \Big] \\
&\quad + \Big[f_k \big(\alpha_k \bar{\gamma}_k (C_1^k)^{-1} + (\alpha_k \bar{\gamma}_k (C_2^k)^{-1} + 1) \big) \\
&\quad \times (Z_2^{-1} L_3(g) L_3(\lambda)^{-1} \gamma_3) \Big] L_k'(\lambda) \\
&\quad + \Big[f_k Z_2^{-1} \big(\gamma_3 L_3(\lambda)^{-1} L_k(\lambda)(\alpha_k \bar{\gamma}_k (C_2^k)^{-1} + 1) \\
&\quad + \alpha_k \bar{\gamma}_k (C_2^k)^{-1} N_k^{-1}(Z_k - 1)Z_1 \lambda_k n_k \gamma_3 \big) \Big] \\
&\quad \times \big(N_1 L_1'(g) + N_2 L_2'(g) \big) \\
&\quad - \big[(\alpha_k \bar{\gamma}_k (C_2^k)^{-1} + 1) f_k L_3(\lambda)^{-2} L_3(g) Z_2^{-1} \gamma_3 L_k(\lambda) \big] \\
&\quad \times \big(N_1 L_1'(\lambda) + N_2 L_2'(\lambda) \big)
\end{aligned}
$$

Defining the coefficients a_0, a_1, a_2, a_3 appropriately this may be written as:

$$
\begin{aligned}
df_k\alpha_k/d\lambda &= a_0 + a_1 L_k'(\lambda) + a_2 \big(N_1 L_1'(g) + N_2 L_2'(g) \big) \\
&\quad + a_3 \big(N_1 L_1'(\lambda) + N_2 L_2'(\lambda) \big)
\end{aligned}
$$

The continuity of the derivatives in the integrand yields:

$$\| L_k^*(\lambda)' \| < \| \int_{\tilde{Z}} a_0 \mu(\tilde{Z}) \|$$

$$+ \| \int_{\tilde{Z}} \Big(a_1 L_k'(\lambda) + a_2 \big(N_1 L_1'(g) + N_2 L_2'(g) \big)$$

$$+ a_3 \big(N_1 L_1'(\lambda) + N_2 L_2'(\lambda) \big) \Big) \mu(\tilde{Z}) \|$$

$$\leq \| \int_{\tilde{Z}} a_0 \mu(\tilde{Z}) \|$$

$$+ K \| \int_{\tilde{Z}} \big(a_1 + (a_2 + a_3)(N_1 + N_2) \big) \mu(\tilde{Z}) \|.$$

Since $\bar{\gamma}_k$ is set arbitrarily in $-1 \leq \bar{\gamma}_k \leq \gamma_k$ it may be chosen such that $1 - \| \int_{\tilde{Z}} \big(a_1 + (a_2 + a_3)(N_1 + N_2) \big) \mu(\tilde{Z}) \| > 0$. Let K be chosen such that:

$$K > \| \int_{\tilde{Z}} a_0 \mu(\tilde{Z}) \| \Big/$$

$$\Big(1 - \| \int_{\tilde{Z}} \big(a_1 + (a_2 + a_3)(N_1 + N_2) \big) \mu(\tilde{Z}) \| \Big),$$

Then $L_k^*(\lambda)'$ is bounded by K if $L_k(\lambda)'$ is, $k = 1, 2$.

To complete the construction of a fixed-point mapping define:

$$\tilde{\phi} = \begin{cases} \phi & \text{if } \phi_k \leq y_k - \beta \ \forall \ k, \ \forall \ \lambda \\ y_k & \text{otherwise.} \end{cases}$$

$$\beta = \text{ a small positive number}$$

It is clear that continuity and boundedness of derivatives is preserved with $\tilde{\phi}$. To show S_k is non-empty let $L_k(\lambda) = \bar{y}$ such that $|y_k - \bar{y}| < \epsilon$ for some arbitrary positive small ϵ. Then $\phi_k(\bar{y}) = \int_{\tilde{Z}} f_k \alpha_k \mu(\tilde{Z})$, $|f_k| < \delta$, $\alpha_k \leq Z_2^{-1} \gamma_3(\lambda) \bar{y}$ and ϕ is arbitrarily small if ϵ is. Therefore $\tilde{\phi} : S_k \times S_k \to S_k \times S_k$.

S_k is closed, bounded and convex. By the Ascoli Theorem continuity and bounded derivatives on each $L \in S_k$ implies S_k is equicontinuous and therefore compact. $\tilde{\phi}$ is a continuous mapping of $S_k \times S_k$ into itself. By the Schauder Fixed Point Theorem $\exists \left(L_1(\lambda), L_2(\lambda)\right) \in S_k \times S_k$ such that $\left(L_1(\lambda), L_2(\lambda)\right) = \phi\left(L_1(\lambda), L_2(\lambda)\right)$. From above, a constant function $\bar{y}$ arbitrarily close to y_k cannot be such an $L_k(\lambda)$. Therefore $\left(L_1(\lambda), L_2(\lambda)\right) = \phi\left(L_1(\lambda), L_2(\lambda)\right)$. By construction aggregate money stock is willingly held and aggregate consumption equals aggregate endowment.

Note that if $\bar{E} \neq E^*$, $\bar{\lambda} \neq \lambda^*$ and therefore $|q_k(t, \bar{E}) - q_k(t, E^*)| \neq 0$. ∎

2. PRICE UNCERTAINTY AND FLEXIBLE EXCHANGE RATES

In Section 1 we presented a paradox. Namely, in a general equilibrium setting that the foreign exchange rate between two competing fiat money assets was indeterminate. This result stemmed from the monies being tied to no particular consumption values and therefore the model was underdetermined. In this section we provide an example of a uniquely determined foreign exchange rate equilibrium. Indeterminacy is overcome by positing future states of the world in which the values of the two monies are unknown. While there are many possible sources of price uncertainty, the example here is perhaps the most straightforward in the sense that the source is left unspecified. However, it should be reiterated that stochastic money stocks are in general insufficient to generate price uncertainty of the kind exhibited here.

A key aspect of the argument is the relation between current exchange rates and prices and possible future events. Here it is assumed that agents know the distribution of future prices. Moreover, expected future exchange rates and prices are permitted to depend in important ways on information which is not easily quantifiable, $e.g.$, the probability of exchange controls. Therefore the model here provides a natural interpretation of seemingly unpredicted exchange rate movement.

2.1 Additional Model Specification.

To highlight our specific point we now make each money stock deterministic and specify the stochastic element in our model as a distribution over price. Let $\{M(t)_i : i = 1, 2\} \equiv \{M_i^0 e^{n_i t} : i = 1, 2\}$. Define the exchange rate under purchasing power parity as $E(t) = P(t)_2 / P(t)_1$ where $P(t)_i$ is the commodity price of money at t. Define states of the world as $\omega \in \Theta$ on the measurable space $(\Theta, \mathcal{F})$ where $\mathcal{F}$ is the σ-field generated by subsets of Θ. Let μ be the probability measure on $\mathcal{F}$. In addition we hold population and income levels constant through time in the analysis of this section. These are assumptions for mathematical simplicity sake only.

Typical agents of country i now solves the choice problem:

$$U^i(\bar{m}(t)_i) = \sup_{C(t)_i} \int_{\Theta} U^i(C(t)_i)\mu(d\omega)$$

subject to: $\quad Y_i - P(t) \cdot m(t)_i - C(t)_{1i} \leq 0$

$$P(t+1) \cdot m(t)_i + c(t)_i - C(t)_{2i} \leq 0$$

where $P(t) = (P(t)_1, P(t)_2)$, $m(t)_i = (m(t)_{i1}, m(t)_{i2})$, $V(t)_i = (C(t)_{1i}, C(t)_{2i})$, $\cdot$ denote inner product, $x(t)_i$ is a real scalar transfer of money i and $m(t)_{ij}$ is the purchase of money j by agent i at time t.

The problem is then written as:

$$U(\bar{m}(t)_i) = \sup_{m(t)_i} \int_{\Theta} U^i\big(Y_i - P(t)\cdot m(t)_i,\, P(t+1)m(t)_i + x(t)_i\big)\mu(d\omega)$$

for an interior solution.

2.2 Temporary Equilibrium.

We suppose that there exists a known distribution of money values at $t+1$ and that the univariate distributions of P_1 and P_2

are not perfectly correlated. It follows that for each ω, in general $P(t+1)_1/P(t+2)_1 \neq P(t+1)_2/P(t+2)_2$ (see Nickelsburg (1984)).

The price vector must satisfy:

$$P(t)_j = \int_\Theta U_2^i P(t+1)_j \mu(d\omega) / \int_\Theta U_1^i \mu(d\omega)$$

$$i, j = 1, 2, \qquad (2.2.4)$$

where U_k^i is the 1st partial derivative with respect to the kth argument.

Foreign exchange rates must satisfy:

$$E(t) = \int_\Theta \nu(t)_i E(t+1) \nu(d\omega), \qquad i = 1, 2.$$

$$\nu(t)_i = U_2^i P(t+1)_1 / \int_\Theta U_2^i P(t+1)_1 \mu(d\omega). \qquad i = 1, 2.$$

THEOREM 2: $\exists$ a vector $\bar{P}(t)$ satisfying (2.2.4) such that $M(t)_i = m(t)_{1i} + m(t)_{2i}$, $C(t)_{11} + C(t-1)_{21} + C(t)_{21} + C(t-1)_{22} = Y_1 + Y_2$ and $E(t)$ is unique.

The proof proceeds by defining the mapping $H : R^4 \to R^4$ by:

$$
\begin{bmatrix}
P(t)_1 \\
P(t)_2 \\
P(t)_1 \cdot m(t)_{11} \\
P(t)_2 \cdot m(t)_{12}
\end{bmatrix}
$$

$$
=
\begin{bmatrix}
\frac{1}{2}\sum_i \int_\Theta U_2^i P(t+1)_1 \mu(d\omega) / \int_\Theta U_1^i \mu(d\omega) \\
\frac{1}{2}\sum_i \int_\Theta U_2^i P(t+1)_2 \mu(d\omega) / \int_\Theta U_1^i \mu(d\omega) \\
\int_\Theta U_2^1 P(t+1)_1 \cdot m(t)_{11} \mu(d\omega) / \int_\Theta U_1^1 \mu(d\omega) \\
\int_\Theta U_2^1 P(t+1)_2 \cdot m(t)_{12} \mu(d\omega) / \int_\Theta U_1^1 \mu(d\omega)
\end{bmatrix}
$$

where $m(t)_1 = \big(M(t)_1 - m(t)_{11},\ M(t)_2 = m(t)_{12}\big)$ is substituted in the arguments of U_j^2, $j = 1, 2$. It is easy to verify that a fixed point of H is an equilibrium vector $\big(m(t)_1, m(t)_2, P(t)\big)$. To compactify the domain choose $\epsilon > 0$ such that $Y_i - P(t) \cdot m(t)_i < \epsilon \Rightarrow \int_\Theta U_2^i P(t+1)_j \mu(d\omega) / \int_\Theta U_1^i \mu(d\omega) < \epsilon$ and $P(t) \cdot m(t)_i < \epsilon \Rightarrow \int U_2^i P(t+1)_j \mu(d\omega) / \int_\Theta U_1^i \mu(d\omega) > \epsilon$. The properties of U insure the existence of such an ϵ. Let $D \equiv \{(P(t), P(t) \cdot m(t)_1) : 0 \leq m(t)_{1j} \leq M(t)_j,\ Y_1 - \epsilon \geq P(t) \cdot m(t)_1 \geq \epsilon,\ j = 1, 2\}$, and define the mapping $\tilde{H} : D \to D$ by:

$$
\tilde{H}(W) = H(W) \quad \text{if } H(x) \in D
$$

$$
\left.
\begin{aligned}
e_k \cdot \tilde{H}(W) &= \epsilon / e_{k+2} \cdot x \\[2mm]
e_{k+2} \cdot \tilde{H}(W) &= \epsilon
\end{aligned}
\right\}
\quad \text{if } e_{k+2} \cdot H(W) < \epsilon, \quad : k = 1, 2
$$

$$e_k \cdot \tilde{H}(W) = (Y_i - \epsilon)/e_{k+2} \cdot x \Big\}$$
$$e_{k+2} \cdot \tilde{H}(W) = (Y_i - \epsilon) \Big\} \quad \text{if } e_{k+2} \cdot H(W) > y_i - \epsilon,$$
$$: k = 1, 2$$

where e_k is a row vector of zeros with 1 in the kth position and $W = (P(t)_1, P(t)_2, m(t)_{11}, m(t)_{12})'$. Continuity of $\tilde{H}$ follows directly from the properties of U, and by construction, elements on the boundary of $\mathcal{D}$ are not fixed points. Moreover $\mathcal{D}$ is convex and compact. Therefore $\exists \bar{W}$ such that $\bar{W} \in \mathcal{D}$ and $\tilde{H}(\bar{W}) = \bar{W}$. Existence follows *mutadis mutandis* through backward recursion from t.

For the uniqueness argument define $(\bar{P}(t), \bar{m}(t)_1)$, $(\hat{P}(t), \hat{m}(t)_1)$ as two equilibria and let $\bar{P} \cdot \bar{m}(t)_1$. It follows that $\hat{C}(t)_{11} > \bar{C}(t)_{11}$ and if $\hat{C}(t)_{21} = \bar{C}(t)_{21}$ then $\bar{P}(t) < \hat{P}(t)$. $\therefore$ The monotonicity of U^j, $j = 1, 2 \Rightarrow \bar{m}(t) \neq \hat{m}(t)$. But $P(t+1) \cdot (\bar{m}(t)_1 + \bar{m}(t)_2) = P(t+1) \cdot (\hat{m}(t)_1 + \hat{m}(t)_2)$, and $\bar{m}(t)_{ij} > \hat{m}(t)_{ij} \Rightarrow \bar{U}_2^i < \hat{U}_2^i$ uniformly in ω. Thus $\bar{P}(t) \cdot \bar{m}(t) > \hat{P}(t) \cdot \hat{(t)} \Rightarrow \int_\Theta \bar{U}_2^1 P(t+1)_j \mu(d\omega) / \int_\Theta \bar{U}_1^1 \mu(d\omega) < \int_\Theta \hat{U}_2^1 P(t+1)_j \mu(d\omega) / \int_\Theta \hat{U}_1^1 \mu(d\omega)$, $j = 1, 2$. Moreover $\int_\Theta \bar{U}_1^2 \mu(d\omega) < \int_\Theta \hat{U}_1^2 \mu(d\omega)$. It follows that if $(\bar{P}(t), \bar{m}(t))$ is a fixed point of H;

$$\int_{\Theta} \hat{U}_2^2 P(t+1)_j \mu(d\omega) \bigg/ \int_{\Theta} \hat{U}_1^2 \mu(d\omega)$$

$$\neq \int_{\Theta} \hat{U}_2^1 P(t+1)_j \mu(d\omega) \bigg/ \int_{\Theta} \hat{U}_1^1 \mu(d\omega)$$

and a contradiction obtains.   ∎

2.3 Remarks.

Demonstrating the result as a temporary equilibrium is not in itself damaging to the argument. This device was chosen for its simplicity, but a full general equilibrium model generates identical conclusions. General equilibrium does require a specification of the source of price uncertainty, and thus, it limits the interest of this example.

The interesting implication of this example is that it is not difficult to resolve the indeterminacy paradox of Kareken and Wallace. What is required, however, is a recognition of the underlying structure which gives rise to the price uncertainty here. This structure effectively differentiates the two monies as assets and may be policy induced or induced by nature.

To establish the policy implication of this result suppose there exists a positive probability π^t of exchange controls being imposed at time t. The exchange control state is one in which the two monies are non-competitive as assets, and therefore price uncertainty of the kind analyzed here obtains. Adding domestic random shocks then makes the model more realistic but does not change its character. In such an environment the money, exchange controls policy can yield counter-intuitive exchange rate movements. (see Nickelsburg (1984))

Finally, this example shows how the introduction of new information and changing, unobserved *future* policy can generate exchange rate movements similar to those observed in the recent floating rates period.

3. A WELFARE ANALYSIS

In this section a managed float regime is analyzed in the context of a stochastic dynamic environment and found to be the appropriate second best optimal regime among the set of regimes considered. This is a comforting result in the sense that such a regime is common practice. Interestingly, the arguments put forth by Friedman in favor of freely flexible exchange rates play an important role in this result.

To begin, let us consider what is known from the above cited research in order to place this section in perspective. The starting point for research in this area is the two papers by Kareken and Wallace. In these, perfect foresight regimes with and without capital controls are analyzed, and of the feasible regimes a co-operatively fixed exchange rate with a constant world money supply is found to be optimal. The stochastic analog of this result for a closed economy is found in Peled (1984). Since such a regime perforce requires economic integration it is not considered to be a practical alternative.

As an alternative Helpman and Razin (1979) assign to money characteristics other than and in addition to the store-of-value characteristic. They find that the way in which their characteristics are specified has a bearing on the desirability of alternative regimes. Helpman goes further in his paper by imposing a Clower constraint on individual economic agents. In Helpman's (1981) model the optimality of alternative regimes is independent of the regime under certain conditions. This is primarily due to the perfect foresight and pure interest arbitrage assumptions. As Helpman suggests, these assumptions are probably critical for the results and therefore a further analysis with weaker assumptions is of interest. We would further suggest that the absence of the Clower constraint or an endogenously derived rather than endogenously imposed Clower constraint would in an uncertain environment overturn these results.

To put this in perspective what is known is the welfare implications of some alternative regimes under perfect foresight with and without Clower constraints, and the welfare implications of particular regimes for small semi-open economies. The models presented here examine stochastic environments including the previously not studied managed float. The impact of capital controls in a large open economy is also reconsidered. There are regimes yet to be considered and some of the results are rather limited. The results that are presented herein do suggest that the intuitive notions of policy makers with respect to freely flexible exchange rates are correct, and that a country ought not rely solely on market forces to set the relative value of its fiat currency.

This section will proceed as follows: in section 3.1 changes in the basic model is set out. Section 3.2 sets out the first important result. A particular managed float regime is shown to be superior to a portfolio autarkic float (complete capital controls). A comparison between tightly managed float regimes and loosely managed float regimes is developed in the fourth section. Section 3.5 discusses and illustrates the welfare implications of 3.3 and 3.4 with respect to various fixed rate regimes, and section 3.6 gives some technical mathematical detail of some proofs.

3.1 Additional Model Specifications.

For our analysis we define alternative environments for the structure of foreign exchange markets. The regimes we consider are defined as:

CF: Co-operative fixed exchange rates

NCF: Non-co-operative fixed exchange rates

FE: Flexible exchange rates

PA: Portfolio autarky

LF: *Laissez faire* in world capital markets

NLF: Managed floating without explicit capital controls.

A regime has two characteristics; a rule for setting exchange rates and a rule for asset trading. The regime is defined as R(.,.), where the two arguments correspond to the two characteristics. The regime R(FE,NLF) may be modified by the degree to which intervention is contemplated by both governments.

Additional Definitions:

$w_{i,j}(t) \equiv$ endowment of goods to the young at time t in country i and state of nature j

$\pi(t) \equiv$ Prob$\{$R(FE,PA) being imposed at time $t+1\}$

$m_j^i(t) \equiv$ holdings of money j by a citizen of country i at time t

$$q_i\big(w_{i,j}(t+1)\big) = \big(x^i(t) + m_i^i(t)\big) P_i(t+1|w_{i,j}(t+1))$$

$r_j \equiv$ Probability of state j in period $t + 1$, $j \in \emptyset$.

DEFINITION: An equilibrium for our expanded model with alternative regimes is a vector $\{C_1^1(t), C_2^1(t), C_1^2(t), C_2^2(t), p_1(t), P_2(t), w_{i,j}(t)\}_{t=0}^{+\infty}$ such that $\forall\ t$:

i) $\sum_i m_j^i(t) = M_j(t)$, $j = 1, 2$

ii) $\sum_i C_1^i(t) N_i + \sum_i C_2^i(t-1) N_i = N_1 w_1(t) + N_2 w_{2,k}(t)$

iii) $U^i\left(C_1^i(t), C_2^i(t)\right) = \max_{m_1^i, m_2^i} \left\{\mathcal{E}_t U^i\left(C_1^i(t), C_2^i(t)\right)\right\}$ subject to R, and $\sum C_1^i(t) = w_{i,j}(t) - \sum P_k(t) m_k^i(t); \sum C_2^i(t) = P_\ell(t+1) m_\ell^i(t) + P_i(t+1)\left(m_i^i(t) + x^i(t)\right)$, $\ell \neq i$.

The above with earlier model assumptions describe the essential structure of the model. Many of the assumptions can be weakened without a loss of the results but these are made solely for the purpose of simplicity. In particular, the specific form of the utility function, constancy of population, small number of contingent endowments, no commodity endowments in the second period, deterministic money stocks and the composite commodity assumption are all stronger than is required. The introduction of a more general structure would increase the mathematical complexity of the model without providing additional insight into the problem.

The notion of optimality is defined in terms of Conditional Pareto Optimality (CPO) and L-Period Conditional Pareto Op-

timality (L-CPO). Allocations $\{\tilde{C}_1^1(t), \tilde{C}_2^1(t), \tilde{C}_1^2(t), \tilde{C}_2^2(t)\}_{t_0}^{+\infty} =$
$\tilde{C}; \{\bar{C}_1^1(t), \bar{C}_2^1(t), \bar{C}_1^2(t), \bar{C}_2^2(t)\}_{T\tau_0}^{+\infty} = \bar{C}$ may be ranked according
to CPS(L-CPS) criteria as follows:

$\bar{C}$ is CPS $\bar{C}$ iff on the set $\{\tilde{C}, \bar{C}\}$, $\tilde{C}$ is CPO and $\bar{C}$ is not
CPO.

$\tilde{C}$ is L-CPS $\bar{C}$ iff on the set $\{\tilde{C}, \bar{C}\}$, $\tilde{C}$ is L-CPO and $\bar{C}$ is not
L-CPO.

DEFINITION: Allocation $\tilde{C}$ is CPO if $\forall\ C^*; \mathcal{E}_t U^i(\tilde{C}^i) \geq$
$\mathcal{E}_t U^i(C^{*i}); \forall\ t, i;$ and $U^i(\tilde{C}_2^i(t_0))$, $i = 1, 2$ with strict inequality for some (i, t).

DEFINITION: Allocation $\tilde{C}$ is L-CPO is $\forall\ C^*; \mathcal{E}_t U^i(\tilde{C}^i) \geq$
$\mathcal{E}_t U^i(C^{*i})$, $\forall\ t \geq t_0 + L$, $i = 1, 2;$ with strict inequality for some
(i, t).

3.2 Risk Sharing and R(FE,PA) Regimes.

This section provides a proof that R(FE,NLF) is conditionally
Pareto Superior to R(FE,PA). The proof proceeds by establishing
conditions under which trade in nominally denominated private
assets between residents of the two countries is welfare improving.
It is then shown that this implies an allocation of consumption
identical to that obtained with R(FE,NLF) and the nominally denominated assets play, in part, the role of trades in the two monies.

Agents in the two countries solve the dynamic optimization problem for R(FE,PA):

$$\max_{m_i^i(t)} \left\{ U^i\left(w_{i,j}(t) - P_i(t, w_{i,j})m_i^i(t)\right) \right.$$

$$\left. + \sum_{j=1}^{K} \gamma_j(t) U^i\left(P_i(t+1, w_{i,j})\left(m_i^i(t) + x^i(t)\right)\right) \right\} \quad (2.3.5)$$

$i = 1, 2; j \in \phi$. A Conditionally Pareto Improving reallocation will be one which increases the maximand for at least one agent and is non-decreasing in the maximand for all agents at all time periods. Define the vector $\delta = (\delta_1, \delta_2)$ as the risk sharing vector and define $N_1\delta_{k,1} = N_2\delta_{k,2} = \delta_k$, $k = 1, 2$. A risk sharing plan is one in which each Country 1 agent receives $\delta_{1,1}$ in one state and $\delta_{2,1}$ in another, while each Country 2 agent receives $-\delta_{1,2}$ in the first state and $-\delta_{2,2}$ in the second. The δ's are denominated in the composite commodity. Without loss of generality, expected utility under risk sharing is:

$$U^i\left(w_{i,j}(t) - P_i(t, w_{i,j})m_i^i(t)\right)$$

$$+ \sum_{j \in \phi^*} \gamma_j(t) U^i\left(P_i(t+1, w_{i,j})(m_i^i(t) + x^i(t))\right)$$

$$+ Y_h(t) U^i\left(P_i(t+1, w_{i,h})(m_i^i(t) + x^i(t)) \pm \delta_{i,1}\right)$$

$$+ y_\ell(t) U^i\left(P_i(t+1, w_{i,\ell})(m_i^i(t) + x^i(t)) \pm \delta_{i,2}\right) \quad (2.3.6)$$

for intra-temporal risk sharing with $\phi^* = \phi - \{h, \ell\}$. For intertemporal risk sharing expected utility with $\phi' = \phi - \{\ell\}$ is:

$$U^i\big(w_{i,j}(t) - P_i(t, w_{i,j})m_i^i(t) \pm \delta_{i,1}\big)$$

$$+ \sum_{j \in \phi'} \gamma_j(t)U^i\Big(P_i(t+1, w_{i,j})\big(m_i^i(t) + x^i(t)\big)\Big)$$

$$\gamma_\ell(t)U^i\Big(P_i(t+1, w_{i,\ell})\big(m_i^i(t) + x^i(t)\big) \pm \delta_{i,2}\Big) \qquad (2.3.7)$$

Define $q_i(w_{i,j}, t) = P_i(t+1, w_{i,j})\big(m_i^i(t) + x^i(t)\big)$ such that q_i is an element of the equilibrium solution to (2.3.5). Substracting (2.3.6) from (2.3.5) and (2.3.7) from (2.3.5) and employing the mean value theorem yields the following sufficient inequalities for welfare improving risk sharing:

$$\gamma_h(t)U^1(X_h)'\delta_{1,1} - \gamma_\ell(t)U^1(X_\ell)'\delta_{2,1} < 0 \qquad (2.3.8)$$

$$-\gamma_h(t)U^2(Y_h)'\delta_{1,2} + \gamma_\ell(t)U^2(Y_\ell)'\delta_{2,2} < 0 \qquad (2.3.9)$$

$$-U^1(X^*)'\delta_{1,1} + \gamma_\ell(t)U^1(X_\ell^*)'\delta_{2,1} < 0 \qquad (2.3.10)$$

$$U^2(Y^*)'\delta_{1,2} - \gamma_\ell(t)U^2(Y_\ell^*)'\delta_{2,2} < 0 \qquad (2.3.11)$$

Inequalities (3.2.4) and (3.2.5) must hold for some (h, P) for intra-temporal risk sharing to be welfare improving, and (3.2.6) and (3.2.7) must hold for some P for intra-temporal risk sharing to be welfare improving. $X_h, X_\ell, Y_h, Y_\ell, X_\ell^*, Y_\ell^*$ are in terms of the second period consumption and X^* and Y^* are in terms of first period consumption, and all (X, Y) variables are given by mean

value theorem. It follows that necessary conditions for the existence of a welfare improving δ vector are:

$$U^1(X_h)'/U^1(X_\ell)' \neq U^2(Y_h)'/U^2(Y_\ell)'$$

or

$$U^1(X^*)'/U^1(X_\ell^*)' \neq U^2(Y^*)/U^2(Y_\ell^*)' \qquad (2.3.12)$$

It will now be shown that the equilibrium solution to agent
problem (2.3.5) under $R(FE, PA)$ yields condition (2.3.12). Without loss of generality let:

$$U^2\big(q_2(w_{2,h}, t)\big)'/U^2\big(q_2(w_{2,\ell}, t)\big)'$$
$$> U^1\big(q_1(w_{1,h}, t)\big)'/U^1\big(q_1(w_{1,\ell}, t)\big)' \qquad (2.3.13)$$

Define δ such that:

$$y_h > q_2(w_{2,h}); \quad Y_\ell < q_2(w_{2,\ell})$$

and

$$X_h < q_1(w_{1,h}); \quad X_\ell > q_1(w_{1,\ell}) \qquad (2.3.14)$$

Then:

$$U^2(Y_h)' < U^2\big(q_2(w_{2,h})\big)';$$
$$U^2(Y_\ell)' > U^2\big(q_2(w_{2,\ell})\big)'$$
$$U^1(X_h)' > U^1\big(q_1(w_{1,h})\big)';$$
$$U^1(X_\ell)' < U^1\big(q_1(w_{1,\ell})\big)' \qquad (2.3.15)$$

Therefore for sufficiently small δ:

$$U^2(Y_h)'/U^2(Y_\ell)' > U^1(X_h)'/U^1(X_\ell)' \qquad (2.3.16)$$

Mutadis mutandis $U^1\big(C_1^1(t)\big)'/U^1(q_1(w_{1,\ell}))' > U^2\big(C_1^2(t)\big)'/$ $U^2\big(q_2(w_{2,\ell})\big)'$ implies the existence of a sufficiently small δ such that (2.3.10) and (2.3.11) hold. For sufficiency notice that (2.3.8) and (2.3.9) and (2.3.10) and (2.3.11) simplify to:

$$\frac{U^1(X_h)'}{U^1(X_\ell)'} < \frac{\gamma_\ell(t)N_1\delta_{2,1}}{\gamma_h(t)N_1\delta_{1,1}} = \frac{\gamma_\ell(t)N_2\delta_{2,2}}{\gamma_h(t)N_2\delta_{1,2}} < \frac{U^2(Y_h)'}{U^2(X_\ell)'} \qquad (2.3.17)$$

$$\frac{U^2(Y^*)'}{U^2(Y_\ell^*)'} < \frac{\gamma_\ell(t)N_2\delta_{2,2}}{N_2\delta_{1,2}} = \frac{\gamma_\ell(t)N_1\delta_{2,1}}{N_1\delta_{1,1}} < \frac{U^1(X^*)'}{U^1(X_\ell^*)'} \qquad (2.3.18)$$

Thus we have the not surprising result that $R(FE, PA)$ yields in general the existence of a welfare improving δ. Let:

$$\begin{bmatrix} \delta_{1,1} \\ \delta_{2,1} \end{bmatrix} = \begin{bmatrix} P_2(t+1,h,\ell)\tau_1(h,\ell) \\ P_2(t+1,h,\ell)\tau_2(h,\ell) \end{bmatrix};$$

$$\begin{bmatrix} \delta_{1,2} \\ \gamma_{2,2} \end{bmatrix} = \begin{bmatrix} P_1(t+1,h,\ell)\tau_2(h,\ell) \\ P_1(t+1,h,\ell)\tau_2(h,\ell) \end{bmatrix} \qquad (2.3.19)$$

It is clear that such vectors exist, and it has been shown that nominally denominated assets $\tau = (\tau_1, \tau_2)$ which may be traded between residents of the two countries can be constructed as risk sharing private debt. Moreover, free trading of τ provides a Conditional Pareto Superior allocation so long as inter- and intra-temporal

MRS's differ between any two agents of the same generation. Such capital flows are prohibited under strict R(FE,PA) regimes.

Now suppose that no prohibition on the trading of τ exists. Then for $\phi = \{1, 2, \ldots, K\}$:

$$P_1(t, w_{i,j}) = \sum_{j \in \phi} \gamma_j(t) \left(U^1 (C_2^1(t))' / \right.$$
$$\left. U^1 (C_1^1(t))' \right) P_1(t + 1, w_{i,j}(t + 1)) \quad (2.3.20)$$

from the optimization problem for Country 1 agents, and:

$$P_2(t, w_{i,j}) = \sum_{j \in \phi} \gamma_j(t) \left(U^1 (C_2^1(t))' / \right.$$
$$\left. U^1 (C_1^1(t))' \right) P_2(t + 1, w_{2,j}(t + 1)) \quad (2.3.21)$$

from the optimization problem for Country 2 agents. But (2.3.16) and (2.3.17) are exactly solutions to the problem:

$$\max_{\delta, m_1^i, m_2^i} \left\{ U^i (w_{i,j} - P_1(t, w_{1,j}) m_1^i(t) - P_2(t, w_{2,j}) m_2^i(t) + \tau_i) \right.$$
$$+ \sum_{j \in \phi} \gamma_j(t) U^i \left(\sum_k P_k(t + 1, j) m_k^i(t) \right.$$
$$\left. + P_i(t + 1, j) x^i(t) + \tau_i(j)) \right\} \quad (2.3.22)$$

subject to aggregate equilibrium conditions on the stocks of $M_1(t)$, $M_2(t)$, and τ. Problem (2.3.22) is the optimization problem solved by agents in R(FE,NLF) with $\pi(t) = 1$. For $|\bar{\pi}(t) - 1| < \nu$ then

$\exists \; \epsilon$ such that $|E_t U^i$ (problem (2.3.22)) $- E_t U^i \big(R(FE, NLF)$:
$\pi(t)) | < \epsilon \; \forall \; \pi(t) \geq \bar{\pi}(t)$. To see this the reader is referred to
Nickelsburg (1984).   The   argument   is   essentially   that
$E_t U^i \big(R(FE, NLF), \pi(t) \big) \quad = \quad \pi(t) E_t U^i (\text{problem} \quad (2.3.22)) +$
$\big(1 - \bar{\pi}(t) \big) U^i \big(C_2^i(t) : R \big(FE, NLF \big)$ in period $t + 1 \big)$. The following
has then been proved:

THEOREM 3: *For the economy defined by a.1-10; R(FE,NLF) is
CPS R(FE,PA).*   ∎

   The intuition behind the argument is that $\pi(t)$ close to 1 corresponds to a tightly managed float. In Nickelsburg (1984) it is
shown that by bounding the exchange rate around the PA exchange rate through selective government intervention (*i.e.*, managing the float) one obtains prices which are arbitrarily close to the
R(FE,PA) equilibrium prices. Thus, by permitting the trading in
nominally dominated assets including money and by managing the
floating exchange rate a Conditionally Pareto Superior allocation
is obtained.

   The meaning of this result is that if countries are unwill-
ing to completely integrate their monetary systems (*i.e.*, to adopt
R(CF,LF)) and do not wish to make the quantity of money endoge-
nous to international events then they are faced with a choice of

R(FE,NLF), R(FE,LF), R(FE,PA), a "crawling peg," R(NCF,LF)

or R(NCF,PA). What has been shown here is that R(FE,NLF) is

Conditionally Pareto Superior to R(FE,PA) for some choices of

$\pi(t)$. Moreover, the floating rate regime of Lapan and Enders has

been shown to be Conditionally Pareto Inferior in general. The

floating rates regimes of Kareken and Wallace are R(FE,LF) and

R(FE,PA). Here it is assumed that R(FE,LF) is not an acceptable

alternative, and the only welfare comparison thus far is the above

result on R(FE,PA). An approximation to R(FE,LF) might be a

loosely managed float (*i.e.*, $\pi(t)$ close to zero). Such a regime will

be studied in the next section.

3.3 Loosely and Tightly Managed Float Regimes.

In this section the question of the appropriate degree of ex-

change market intervention is taken up. To be sure, intervention

may be of many forms, and consequently only a subset of interven-

tion policies are considered here. We consider the tightly managed

float, defined as a policy which keeps exchange rates close to the

asset autarky or trade determined exchange rate (as in Section

3.2), and the loosely managed float, defined as a policy which at

some time in the very distant future fixes the range of the exchange

rate but is otherwise a *laissez-faire* policy. A strictly *laissez-faire*

policy is not examined because of the non-uniqueness of equilib-

rium with fiat money as defined here; however, the loosely managed float bears a strong resemblance to a *laissez-faire* equilibrium,
and the policy serves as a selection device for choosing one of the
equilibria. Thus the loose float corresponds to what is ordinarily
referred to as a *laissez-faire* floating regime.

With a model employing non-specific functional forms for the
utility functions of agents as are employed here, strong welfare
results are not generally expected. It is no surprise then that the
results here are somewhat weak. Specifically, unambiguous conditional superiority for all points in time is not found, nor are
interventionist policies that lie between the loose and tight policies defined here considered rigorously. The results here do lead
to interesting descriptions of the potential gains and losses from
exchange market intervention and suggest the possibility of poten-
tially welfare improving (for one country) policy games. Moreover,
they suggest strongly the inability to achieve a sustainable welfare
game through quasi-*laissez-faire* policies.

To be specific, define the R(FE,NLF) tightly managed float
as a regime with the sequence $\{\pi(t)\}$ defined as $\pi(t) \doteq 1 \ \forall \ t \geq t_0$.
Equilibria to be considered will be those for which R(FE,NLF) is
continued for all future t. All variables associated with this regime
will be denoted by a " ˆ ". The R(FE,NLF) loosely managed float

is defined by:

i) $E(T,j) = \xi_j \bar{E}(T,j)$ $j = 1, 2 \ldots, K$

ii) $\xi_j < +\infty$

iii) $\pi(t) \doteq 0$ $t < T$.

It should be noted that in this regime the ξ_j are constants independent of time while the T is a variable that may be progressively increased. All variables associated with this regime are denoted by an "*". The time independence requirement placed on the ξ_j is simply a requirement that at time T one of the two countries cannot force a hyperinflation on the other country by changing the exchange rate intervention policy.

Consider an ith country individual. The difference in expected utility from the two regimes is:

$$
U^i\left(w_{i,\ell}(t) - \sum_k \hat{P}_k(t)\hat{m}_k^i(t)\right) - U^i\left(w_{i,\ell}(t) - \sum_k P_k^*(t)m_k^{*i}(t)\right)
$$
$$
+ \sum_j \gamma_j(t)\Big[U^i\Big(\hat{P}_i(t+1:j)(\hat{m}_i^i(t) + x^i(t))
$$
$$
+ \hat{P}_n(t+1:j)(\hat{m}_n^i(t) + \hat{t}_i(t:j))\Big)
$$
$$
- U^i\Big(P_i^*(t+1:j)(m_i^{*i}(t) + x^i(t))
$$
$$
+ P_n^*(t+1:j)(m_n^{*i}(t) + \tau_i^*(t:j))\Big)\Big] \tag{2.3.23}
$$

where $i, k, \ell, n \in \{1, 2\}$. $n \neq i$, $j \in \phi$. Employing the mean value theorem and aggregating over generation t citizens of country i

yields the necessary and sufficient condition for a R^* regime to be conditionally Pareto superior for generation t, country i agents:

$$N_i \sum_i \hat{P}_k(t)\hat{m}_k^i(t) - N_i \sum_k P_k^*(t)m_k^{*i}(t)$$

$$> N_i \sum_j \gamma_j(t)\left(U^i(Y_{i,j})'/U^i(X_{i,j})'\right)\left[\sum_k \hat{P}_k(t+1:j)\hat{m}_k^i(t)\right.$$

$$- \sum_k P_k^*(t+1:j)m_k^{*i}(t) + x^i\left(\hat{P}_i(t+1:j) - P_i^*(t+1:j)\right)$$

$$\left. + \hat{P}_n(t+1:j) - P_n^*(t+1:j)\tau_i^*(t:j)\right] \qquad (2.3.24)$$

To establish the truth or falsity of (3.3.2) requires the description of the $*$ and $\hat{}$ equilibria. The $\hat{}$ is identical in prices to that of the trade determined equilibrium described in Section 3.2. The value of the two monies is a function of the rate of expansion of the two money stocks. Thus, for example $\hat{P}_1(t) = (Z_1^{t-t_0})^{-1}\hat{P}_1(t_0)$. Differences in the rates of return for the two monies persist because of the different rates of return in the possible autarkic state. The loose float, because of the low probability of intervention forces the rates of return on the two monies to be more nearly equal. It is this fact which gives rise to the main results of this section.

The heuristic argument is that if the rates of return are on average equal, the money of Country 1 must depreciate (appreciate) in value more rapidly (slowly) than under the $\hat{}$ regime ($Z_2 > Z_1$). Were this not so the value of Country 2's money would soon exceed the value of the commodity endowment. Thus less favorable intertemporal trades are presented to model agents, and with the same value for second period endowments these agents achieve lower utility. It may be the case that second period endowments actually increase in value. The issue then centers on the value of these transfers (taxes) of money.

In Section 3.6, the mathematical appendix it is shown that the value of transfers in Country 2 money must be smaller under the "*" regime. The value of transfers in Country 1 money may rise initially, but the faster (slower) rate of depreciation (appreciation) implies that ultimately these endowments must also decline in value. The duration of this possible welfare increasing period for Country 1 agents depends crucially on the relative difference in Country 1 and 2 money growth rules.

Finally, whether Country 1 agents are actually better off for a finite period of time under the "*" regime is as yet not known. The conjecture is that such an increase in welfare, if it exists at all is not a general case and is of short duration. Formally:

THEOREM 4: *In the economy described by a.1=a.6, and $Z_2 > Z_1$:*

$\exists\, t^{**} \geq t_0,\ t^{**} < +\infty$ *such that* $\forall\, t \geq t^{**} (\mathcal{E}_t \hat{U}^1) > (\mathcal{E}_t U^1)^*$; *and*

$\forall\, t \geq t_0 (\mathcal{E}_t \hat{U}^2) > (\mathcal{E}_t U^2)^*$.

Theorem 4 states that the tightly managed float is L-CPS
to the loosely managed float. Therefore, Country 1 may obtain
some welfare gain from having a loosely managed float but such
a gain will be completely dissipated in finite time, and thereafter
there will be an unambiguous decline in welfare. Country 2 cannot
obtain any welfare gain with a loosely managed float.

The obvious questions that arise at this juncture are why
doesn't one consider a loosely managed float until t^{**} and a tightly
managed one thereafter? And suppose Country 1 agents have a
very high discount rate, then is not a loosely managed float better?
The answer to the first question revolves around the construction
of the equilibrium. If a policy change occurs t^{**} then the entire
equilibrium path will be changed. Hence the old t^{**} is no longer
the relevant policy change time. A backward recursion argument
will demonstrate that if such a policy is planned the elements giv-
ing rise to the possible welfare improvement are no longer relevant,
and indeed, the loosely managed float disappears. For the second
question, consider the myopic policy makers at t^{**} searching for
optimal policies. The loosely managed float is no longer attractive
relative to the tight float, and by backward recursion again the optimal myopic policy gives rise to something other than the loosely
managed float and more akin to the tightly managed float. Thus

one either has a loosely managed float as defined here or some other regime, but the properties of the float cannot be exploited without changing the nature of the regime and the concommitant equilibria.

This is not to argue that some middle ground policy is not possibly a better alternative, at least for some countries. There is much room for further exploration and study of hybrid regimes. It is conjectured on the basis of the results here that a hybrid policy given Z_1 and Z_2 would at best serve to redistribute world real income from agents in one country to agents in the other country, and therefore such a policy would not be a Nash policy in the space of two country policies.

3.4 A Word on Fixed Exchange Rates.

In this study a detailed examination of fixed rate regimes is not provided; in part because the main results are already known and to rediscover them would be redundant and in part because some alternative fixed rate regimes map very nicely into regimes studied in Section 4. The two issues that require further eluci- dation and perspective, and are the subject of this section, are optimality and feasibility.

First consider a $R(CF,\cdot)$ regime. The results here and in Kareken and Wallace (1977) clearly indicate that blocking in-

tertemporal trade in assets is suboptimal. Thus, R(CF,LF) is the
CPS regime, but is it a reasonable alternative? Kareken and Wallace, and Peled make a strong case for the optimality of a constant
money stock regime in a country with one money. One means of
attaining R(CF,LF) is to engage in co-operation in the setting of
world, rather than domestic, money growth targets. Thus the en-
dogeneity of domestic money stocks follows, and the constancy of
$M_1(t) + EM_2(t)$ is the CPO policy. The difficulty with such a policy is that it involves the substantial integration of two economies,
which on non-economic grounds may not be the most desirable
policy. One need only witness the difficulty encountered in attempting to affect this kind of policy co-ordination in the E.E.C.
to understand that substantial monetary integration between two
countries (*e.g.*, France and West Germany) is not often viewed by
either as welfare improving. This seems to hold in spite of solid
economic arguments to the contrary.

For small open economies the case may not be so clear, and
Lapan and Enders (1980) provide some evidence on this. Their
results are for a R(NCF,PA) economy and it seems clear that CPS
policies can be implemented. Furthermore, if the domestic money
stock is not to be a random variable, other exchange control is
necessary for the Lapan and Enders economy to be sustainable.

So, while this small country example remains to be fully worked out with a CPO criterion, the maintenance of an R(NCF,·) regime implies either a random $M(t)$ or further restriction of individual choice. Neither of these characteristics usually engender Pareto improving allocations in economic models.

What then are the alternatives? The two that appear most obvious, and for which there are actual historical examples, are those which allow for a crawling band on exchange rate for adjustments to differential monetary policies; and to co-operatively agree to fix the exchange rate at some time in the future in a way so as not to differ too much from the pure trade exchange rate. These two alternative regimes are identical in form to the regimes studied in Section 3.3. If the co-operative regime implies a *laissez-faire* environment then the equilibrium is the same as the loosely managed float. If the crawling band bounds the exchange rate around the autarkic rate then the tightly managed float obtains. Other structures for these fixed exchange rate regimes fall between these two cases, and aside from cross-country transfers of income, not much can be said as yet of them. Therefore, among the fixed rate regimes, one is forced to consider only second best policies as a practical matter. These second best policies appear to engender the CPO and L-CPO results of Sections 3 and 4.

3.5 Concluding Remarks.

The above exercise characterizes the welfare implications of alternative exchange rate regimes. It is a well known result that a single world money stock, and by implication a co-operatively fixed exchange rate, will under certain conditions insure optimality in the CPO sense. However, this policy, while attractive from an economics point of view is not very practical. Barring such a policy one must be concerned with the impact of capital flows and the tenuousness of monetary equilibrium.

The central result of the paper is that the tightly managed floating exchange rate regime provides roughly a CPO regime. It accomplishes this by neutralizing the effect of capital flows on the exchange rate and rate of return on money holdings will not prevent any mutually advantageous exchanges. Thus, the Friedman argument for flexible exchange rates, autonomy of domestic monetary policy and insulation against foreign exogenous shocks, hold as an argument for a tightly managed float. The argument does not hold for other exchange rate regimes.

The second main point of this paper is the demonstration that particular exchange rate policies may increase the individual welfare of citizens of one country at the expense of non-citizens. This opens the question of optimal Nash equilibrium policies which is not explored. It is shown that for a set of these policies, namely loosely managed float regimes, to the extent that any one country's citizens gain from the policies it is not a sustainable gain. Indeed, in finite time the effect of such a policy is to make everyone from that time forward in all countries worse off by the CPO criterion. Thus, another interesting extension would be to explore the extent to which myopic decision makers will be led to induce an increase in the utility of presently alive citizens at the expense of other country citizens and own country future generations. Of particular interest here would be to consider many period lived generations under assumptions about future regime changes in response to a degradation of individual welfare.

Finally, a caveat bears repetition. This work examines a particular aspect of the optimal exchange rate problem. The regimes considered are those most often taken up in the literature, but by no means do they constitute an exhaustive set. This work may then best be viewed as providing a set of results on individual welfare and optimal exchange rate regimes from which other elaborations and extensions ought to be developed toward the goal of a taxomony of welfare results over all possible regimes.

3.6 Mathematical Appendix.

It was shown in Nickelsburg (1980), Proposition II that a $R(FE, LF)$ regime (*i.e.*, $\pi(t) = 0 \; \forall \; t$) has an indeterminate equilibrium. To resolve the indeterminacy an NLF regime is posited with $E(T, j)$ given for T large, $\forall \; j \in \phi$.

DEFINITION: Regime $R^*(FE, NLF)$ is defined as $R(FE, NLF)$ with $\{\pi(t)\}_{t_0}^{T-1} = 0$ and $\{E(T, j); j \in \phi\}$, T large. Variables associated with R^* will be denoted by "$*$" superscript. Regime $\hat{R}(FE, NLF)$ is defined as $R(FE, NLF)$ with $\{\pi(t)\}_{t_0}^{T} = 1$. Variables associated with $\hat{R}$ will be denoted by a circumflex.

LEMMA 1: *In the economy defined by a.1-a.10 and $\hat{R}$;*

    i) $\hat{E}(t) \doteq \bar{E}(t)$

    ii) $\hat{P}_i(t) \doteq \bar{P}_i(t), \quad i = 1, 2$

with $\bar{X}$ a variable defined by the equilibrium value of $R(FE, PA)$.

PROOF: Immediate from (2.3.20) and (2.3.21). ∎

LEMMA 2: *In the economy defined by a.1-a.10 and R^*;*

    i) $E(t, j) \in [\min\{E^*(T)\}, \max\{E^*(T)\}] \; \forall \; (t \leq T), (j \in \phi)$.

    ii) $\forall \; \{P_i(t)\} \; \not\exists$ *a subsequence* $\{P_i(t_j)\}, t_j \in \{t_1, t_2, \ldots\}$ *such that* $P_i(t_j)/P_i(T_{j-1}) > (Z_2^{-1})^{t_j - t_{j-1}}$.

PROOF: Let $j, \ell, k \in \{1, 2, \ldots, K\}$, $i \in \{1, 2\}$. Given state ℓ at time $t - 1$ define the function $v_i(\ell, t, j) : R^{3K} \to R^1$, the matrix

$V_i(t)$ and the vector $E(t)$ by:

$$v_i(\ell,t,j) = \left(U^i(C_2^i(t-1;j))'\gamma_j(t-1)P_1(t,j)\right)$$
$$\div \sum_k \left(U^i(C_2^i(t-1,k))'\right.$$
$$\left. \times \gamma_k(t-1)P_1(t,k)\right) \qquad (2.3.25)$$

$$V_i(t) = \begin{bmatrix} v_i(1,t,1) & v_i(1,t,2) & \cdots & v_i(1,t,K) \\ v_i(2,t,1) & & & \\ \vdots & & & \\ v_i(K,t,1) & & \cdots & v_i(K,t,K) \end{bmatrix} \qquad (2.3.26)$$

$$E(t) = \text{Transpose}[E(t,1), E(t,2), \ldots, E(t,K)] \qquad (2.3.27)$$

Define the function $V_i^*(t) : R^{K^2} \times R^{K^2} \to R^{K^2}$ by:

$$V_i^*(t) = V_i(t) \cdot V_i^*(t+1) \qquad (2.3.28)$$

At, T, $E(T)$ is fixed by assumption. Maximization of (2.3.22) yields:

$$E(t-1) = V_i(T-1)E(T) \qquad (2.3.29)$$

Backward recursion on a.7 to time t yields:

$$E(t) = V_i^*(t)E(T) \qquad (2.3.30)$$

Now $\sum_j v(\ell,t,j) = 1, = v(\ell,t,j) > 0; \forall \ell, t, j$. It follows that

$$E(t,j) \in (\min\{E(T,j)\}, \max\{E(t,j)\}). \qquad (2.3.31)$$

$$[\min\{E(t,j)\}, \max\{E(t,j)\}]$$

$$\subset [\min\{E(t+1,j)\}, \max\{E(t+1,j)\}], \ \forall \, t < T \quad (2.3.32)$$

$M_2(t) = M_2(t_0)Z^{t-t_0}$ by assumption. Suppose $\exists$ a sequence $\{P_2(t)\}$ which has a subsequence $\{P_2(t_i)\}$ such that

$$P_2(t_i)/P_2(t_{i-1}) = (\delta_2 Z_2^{-1})^{t_i - t_{i-1}}$$

$$> (Z_2^{-1})^{t_i - t_{i-1}}; \qquad t_i \in \{t_1, t_2, \ldots\}$$

Then $P_2(t_i)M_2(t_i) = P_2(t_0)M_2(t_0)\delta_2^{t_i - t_0}$. It follows that $P_2(t_i)$ $\times M_2(t_i) \to +\infty$ as $T \to +\infty$, $t_i \to +\infty$. $\therefore \forall \{P_2(t)\} \not\exists$ a subsequence $\{P_2(t_i)\}$.

Suppose $\exists$ a sequence $\{P_1(t)\}$ which has a subsequence $\{P_1(t_j)\}$ such that

$$P_1(t_j)/P_1(t_{j-1}) = (\delta_1 Z_2^{-1})^{t_j - t_{j-1}}$$

$$> (Z_2^{-1})^{t_j - t_{j-1}}, \qquad t_j \in \{t_1, t_2, \ldots\}$$

Then $E(t_j) = P_2(t_j)/P_1(t_j) < (\delta_1^{t_j - t_0})^{-1}$. It follows that $E(t_j) \to 0$ as $T \to +\infty$, $t_i \to +\infty$. $\therefore \forall \{P_1(t)\} \not\exists$ a subsequence $\{P_1(t_j)\}$.   ∎

LEMMA 3: $\exists \, t^{**} < +\infty$ and $T^{**} < +\infty$ such that $\forall \, t > t^{**}$, $T > T^{**}$:

i) $P_1^*(t)M_1(t) + P_2^*(t)M_2(t) < \hat{P}_1(t)M_1(t) + \hat{P}_2(t)M_2(t)$

ii) $P_i^*(t) < \hat{P}_i(t)$

PROOF: $\hat{P}_1(t) = (Z_1^{t-t_0})^{-1}\hat{P}_1(t_0)$ and $\hat{P}_2(t) = (Z_2^{t-t_0})^{-1}\hat{P}_2(t_0)$ by Nickelsburg (1984), Proposition 4. Suppose $\nexists\, T^*$ such that $\forall\, t > T^*$, $P_i^*(t) \leq (Z_2^{t-t_0})^{-1}P_i^*(t_0)$. Then $\exists$ a sequence of integers $\{t_1, t_2, \ldots\}$ such that $P_i^*(t_j) > (Z_2^{t-t_0})^{-1}P_i^*(t_0)\ \forall\, t_j \in \{t_1, t_2, \ldots\}$ which contradicts Lemma 2.

Then $P_1^*(t)M_1(t) + P_2^*(t)M_2(t) \leq \big(P_1^*(t_0)M_1(t) + P_2^*(t_0) \times M_2(t)\big)(Z_2^{t-t_0})^{-1}$ and $\hat{P}_1(t)M_1(t) + \hat{P}_2(t)M_2(t) = \hat{P}_1(t_0)M_1(t) \times (Z_1^{t-t_0})^{-1} + \hat{P}_2(t_0)M_2(t)(Z_2^{t-t_0})^{-1}$. $\therefore\ P_1^*(t)M_1(t) + P_2^*(t) \times M_2(t) < \hat{P}_1(t)M_1(t) + \hat{P}_2(t)M_2(t)$ if $P_1^*(t_0)M_1(t) + P_2^*(t_0)M_2(t) < \hat{P}_1(t_0)M_1(t)(Z_1^{t-t_0}) + \hat{P}_2(t_0)M_2(t_0)$. $(Z_1^{t-t_0})^{-1}(Z_2^{t-t_0}) \to +\infty$ as $t \to +\infty$. $\therefore\ \exists\, T'$ such that $\forall\, t > T' \sum_k P_k^*(t)M_k(t) < \sum_k \hat{P}_k(t)M_k(t)$.

$P_1^*(t) \leq (Z_2^{t-t_0})^{-1}P_1^*(t_0)$ and $\hat{P}_1 = (Z_1^{t-t_0})^{-1}\hat{P}_1(t_0)$. $\therefore Z_2 > Z_1 \Rightarrow \exists\, T''$ such that $P_1^*(t) < \hat{P}_1(t)\ \forall\, t > T''$. $E^*(t) < \xi\bar{E}(T)$ by Lemma 1. Further $\bar{E}(t) > \bar{E}(t+1)$ and $\bar{E}(t) \to 0$ as $t \to +\infty$ by Nickelsburg (1984), Proposition 4. $\therefore \exists\, T'''$ such that $\forall\, T > T''' \hat{E}(T) > \xi\bar{E}(T) > E^*(t)$. $\therefore \forall\, t > T'' P_2^*(t) < \hat{P}_2(t)$.

Let $t^{**} = \max\{T', T''\}$ and $T^{**} = T'''$. ∎

PROOF OF THEOREM 4: From Lemma 3 $\forall\, t > t^{**}$, $c_2^{*1}(t) + C_2^{*2}(t) < \hat{C}_2^1(t) + \hat{C}_2^2(t)$; $P_1^*(t)X^1(t-1) < \hat{P}_1(t)X^1(t-1)$ and $P_2^*(t)X^2(t-1) < \hat{P}_2(t)X^2(t-1)$. Define $f_j^i(\cdot) = U^i(C_1^i(t) :$

$w_{i,k}(t))'/U^i\big(C_2^i(t) \,:\, w_{i,j}(t+1)\big)'$; $\hat{x}^i = \big(\hat{C}_1^i(t), \hat{C}_2^i(t)\big)$; $x^{*i} = \big(C_1^{*i}(t), C_2^{*i}(t)\big)$ and $y^i = (X_i, Y_i)$ where the elements of y^i are defined by (2.3.24). From the first order conditions for (2.3.22):

$$\sum_{j\in\phi} \gamma_j(t) f_j^1(\hat{x}^1)^{-1} \big(\hat{P}_1(t+1)/\hat{P}_1(t)\big)$$
$$= \sum_{j\in\phi} \gamma_j(t) f_j^1(x^{*1})^{-1} \big(P_1^*(t+1)/P_1^*(t)\big)$$
$$= \sum_{j\in\phi} \gamma_j(t) f_j^2(\hat{x}^2)^{-1} \big(\hat{P}_1(t+1)/\hat{P}_1(t)\big)$$
$$= \sum_{j\in\phi} \gamma_j(t) f_j^2(x^{*2})^{-1} \big(P_1^*(t+1)/P_1^*(t)\big) \qquad (2.3.33)$$

Assumption a.5, Lemma 3 and (3.6.9) imply $C_2^{*1}(t) < \hat{C}_2^1(t)$ and $C_2^{*2}(t) < \hat{C}_2^2(t)$. Similarly from the first order conditions for (2.3.22):

$$\sum_k \hat{P}_k(t)\hat{m}_k^i(t) - \sum_k P_k^*(t)m_k^*(t)$$
$$= \sum_j \gamma_j(t)[f_j^i(\hat{x}^i)^{-1} \sum_k \hat{P}_k(t+1)\hat{m}_k^i(t)$$
$$- f_j^k(x^{*i}) \sum_k P_k^*(t+1)m_k^{*i}(t)] \qquad (2.3.34)$$

Lower second period consumption, a.5 and the mean value theorem imply

$$f_j^i(\hat{x}^i) < f_j^i(y^i) < f_j(x^{*i})$$

$$\therefore \quad \sum_k \hat{P}_k(t)\hat{m}_k^i(t) - \sum_k P_k^*(t)m_k^{*i}(t)$$

$$< \sum_j \gamma_j(t)f_j^i(y^i)[\sum_k \hat{P}_k(t+1)\hat{m}_k^i(y) - \sum_k P_k^*(t+1)m_k^{*i}(t)]$$

$$+ x^i(t)(\hat{P}_i(t+1) - P_i^*(t+1))$$

which is condition (2.3.24) for the CPS of a tightly managed float
for $t > t^{**}$.   ∎

REFERENCES

Bental, B., 1979, Capital controls in a two sector model of growth and trade, Ph.D. Thesis, University of Minnesota.

Helpman, E. 1981, An exploration in the theory of exchange rate regimes, *Journal of Political Economy* 89, 865-890.

Helpman, E. and A. Razin, 1979, Towards a consistent comparison of alternative exchange rate systems, *Canadian Journal of Economics*, 394-409.

Kareken, J. and N. Wallace, 1977, Portfolio autarky: a welfare analysis, *Journal of International Economics* 7, 19-43.

Kareken, J. and N. Wallace, 1981, On the indeterminacy of equilibrium exchange rates, *Quarterly Journal of Economics*, 96, 207-222.

Lapan, H.E. and W. Enders, 1980, Random disturbances and the choice of exchange regimes in an intergenerational model, *Journal of International Economics* 10, 263-283.

Nickelsburg, G., 1980, On the multiplicity of stochastic dynamic exchange rate equilibrium, Modelling Research Group working paper no. 8032, Department of Economics, University of Southern California.

Nickelsburg, G., 1984, Dynamic exchange rate equilibria with uncertain government policy, *Review of Economic Studies* LI, 509-519.

Peled, D., 1984, Stationary Pareto optimiality of stochastic asset equilibria with overlapping generations, *Journal of Economic Theory* 34, 396-403.

Samuelson, P.A., 1958, An exact consumption-loan model of interest with or without the social contrivence of money, *Journal of Political Economy* 66, 467-482.

CHAPTER 3

Empirical Implementation of
the Instability Hypothesis

1. INSTABILITY AND THEORETICAL MODELS

In the previous chapter we saw that general equilibrium models could be constructed in a natural way to yield seemingly unstable exchange rate equilibrium. These equilibria were difficult to describe in an empirically satisfactory way and were constrained by the simplicity of the model to show somewhat specific behavior. While this was the intention of the exercise, we wish to go beyond those models to a less restrictive modelling format which will guide our empirical work. It is important to keep in mind the previous results as they will set the stage for the model construction and theory of this chapter. To begin with we return to the more traditional currency substitution literature of Calvo and Rodriguez (1977) and Canto and Nickelsburg (1984a,1984b) and review briefly the literature which we adopt to fit the results of Chapter 2.

The previous literature on instability in foreign exchange markets has focused on three aspects of alternative exchange rate regimes. First, there is a literature on speculation in foreign exchange markets in which the exchange rate is fixed by the operation of buffer stocks, or through the use of controls. Examples of this work are Krugman (1979), Flood and Garber (1981), and Salant (1983). The basic ideas of this literature is to show how speculative attacks may occur in asset markets. Recurrent foreign exchange crises are then associated with speculative attacks on a currency. Other successful applications of this framework include: 1) the analysis of a collapse of the banking system, Garber (1981) and 2) the study of the sudden monetary contraction which would result if an attack terminated a government attempt to monetize gold, Flood and Garber (1982).

A second strand in the instability literature seeks to elucidate the "vicious circle" view of foreign exchange markets. Recall that the basic point of this literature is that short term asset market disturbances feed into exchange rates and domestic prices, and these disturbances can induce wage-price spirals and exchange rate depreciation processess. (See Bavesi and De Grauwe (1977).) In this view foreign exchange markets are not globally stable and the instability provides an explanation for a portion of LDC inflation.

(For a discussion of these issues see Bilson (1979).)

Finally there is the literature on saddle path instability in dynamic perfect foresight models which include currency substitution models. Brock (1974,1975) has examined the possible equilibria in these models, and for certain cases, ruled out the possibility that dynamically unstable paths will be followed by an economy. Further attempts to provide justification for the saddle path assumption are provided by Lucas (1975), Kouri (1976), Fischer (1979). Obstfeld and Rogoff (1983) re-examined Brock's claim and found it not completely general. In their model a consistent optimizing path can have the value of money asymptotically zero. While one might argue about the appropriateness of such an unstable price path for closed and for large economies, in the open-small economy setting the possibility of substitution away from the use of domestic money by domestic residents is more appealing.

A natural question raised by an attempt to apply these models to actual phenomena and raised earlier in this volume is will the local government permit its currency to be driven out of existence? If the answer is no, as we argued in the previous chapter, then the question becomes, how does the local government prevent complete substitution and how do such policies affect equilibrium paths of exchange rates? In what follows we answer these questions once again and in somewhat the same way but with a simpler framework.

In our analysis the government exogenously selects a money growth rate. To insure its currency remains attractive, contingency controls on foreign money acquisition and on the repatriation of foreign source interest earnings are designed. The two controls envisaged, a flow, foreign exchange tax and a stock, foreign asset tax are the controls most frequently observed. Appropriately designed, these controls have the effect of moderating, stopping or even reversing the flight into foreign money and if applied only when the terms of trade changes or capital flows become large can generate cycles of free trade and exchange alternating with exchange market controls.

The types of controls we are describing make it more costly to substitute foreign for domestic money accounts. These controls include restrictions on imports and multi-tiered exchange rate systems that limit the conversion of the earnings of foreign exchange so as to diminish the real value of foreign money, and include measures to make illegal or subject to tax foreign currency holding. We try to capture this by modelling their unifying aspect, namely they each raise the cost of holding foreign money.

In the next sections we describe our candidate empirical

model and present an analysis of equilibrium paths which include recurrent crises. In the final section we illustrate the use of our approach to interpret exchange rate phenomena for the Dominican Republic.

2. MODELLING CONSIDERATIONS

We begin our modelling by adopting the formal structure of currency substitution in Calvo and Rodriguez (1977). Our motivation is to have a flexible, stylized model of currency substituion which will permit both stable and unstable dynamic paths. Following Calvo and Rodriguez (CR) we model a small open economy. We assume that "open" implies that the market sector of the economy is in large part dominated by international transactions, and thus foreign currency is available as a substitute money. Moreover, domestic residents must continually be aware of the value of some foreign currency (*e.g.*, U.S. dollars) even if they do not transact in it and the substantial foreign trade sector gives them, in the absense of government controls, access to the foreign currency. Because the economy is small and open its money is assumed for convenience not to be considered an asset by foreign citizens. Under these assumptions, the free market existence of a positive equilibrium price of the domestic money is tenuous and the stability of such an equilibrium cannot be assumed *a priori*.

In the last chapter we showed that the idea that currency substitution may engender possible instability has some basis in optimizing models. When carried *to its limit*, perfect substitution, we have found that the exchange rate will not be determined by competitive markets. Government intervention through institutional arrangements, (*e.g.*, legal tender laws and gold-clause laws), or through market controls, (*e.g.*, capital controls, bank deposit controls and multi-tiered exchange rates), will of course prevent the perfect substitutability of the two monies. However, these controls increase the cost of international transactions and are generally employed only in times of crises. Consequently we suggest that the unstable region of the CR model may well characterize the dynamics of an economy in the absense of currency controls or during the lifting of currency controls.

We construct our analysis under the assumption that for seignorage reasons governments will not choose to abandon their own currency. while they may avoid a run on the currency by reform of monetary policy or international co-ordination of exchange regimes, they typically employ exchange and capital controls.

When one begins with the premise of unstable markets, direct controls though partially circumvented can play an important role in maintaining a positive price for an otherwise unwanted currency. Moreover the implementation of controls may give rise to interesting exchange rate and control dynamics.

For example, in many of the Latin American countries, where governments frequently impose exchange controls, it is believed that the effect is to increase the inflation tax base over and above what would have otherwise existed. Thus, the dynamic interchange between the price of money and controls may well explain periodic exchange crises in these countries. Also, the recently discussed vicious-cycle hypothesis which seems to have some empirical validity, though this is still not clear, but which has been ruled out in other theoretical models in the absence of accommodating monetary policy, reappears in our model as a theoretical possibility in its own right. The reason is that even if the government holds the nominal quantity of domestic money constant, perceived long run depreciation of domestic currency value can lead to the substitution of foreign currency in domestic transactions and create self fulfilling price-exchange rate cycles.

3. THE MODEL

Our economy is a two sector small open economy. One sector produces an internationally traded good whose foreign price, P_T, is determined in the world market. The other sector produces a nontraded good, whose price in domestic currency, P_H, is determined by domestic demand and supply conditions. Full price flexibility is assumed and the relative price of the traded good in terms of the nontraded good, e, is expressed as:

$$e = \frac{EP_T}{P_H} \qquad (3.3.1)$$

where E denotes the nominal exchange rate between domestic and foreign currencies. Domestic and foreign currencies are the only available assets since we are only interested in the substitution between them. For simplicity we set the foreign price $P_T = 1$, although for empirical work changes in foreign price levels need to be accounted for.

Given factor endowments, rates of consumption and production of traded and nontraded goods are assumed to depend on levels of domestically owned real wealth (a) and the relative prices faced by domestic consumers and producers. With full price flexibility, equilibrium in the market for home goods must always prevail, which we write as:

$$H(a, e) = 0; \quad H_a > 0; \qquad H_e > 0. \qquad (3.3.2)$$

The only way for our economy to alter the level of its foreign currency holdings is through an excess supply or demand of traded goods. Since excess demands are functions of domestically owned wealth and the relative price of the two goods it follows that in equilibrium

$$\frac{dR}{dt} = \dot{R} = -F(a,e), \quad F_a > 0, \quad F_e < 0, \tag{3.3.3}$$

where $-F$ denotes the small open economy net export function and R is the total stock of domestic holdings of foreign currency. The real value of assets in terms of the home good is defined as:

$$a = m + eR \tag{3.3.4}$$

where $m = M/P_H$ is the real value of domestic currency. Our assumptions about the sign of the partial derivatives in equations (3.3.2) and (3.3.3) implies a negative relationship between the stock of assets and the relative price faced by domestic producers and consumers. Following CR, from equation (3.3.2) there exists a function v such that:

$$a = v(e) \tag{3.3.5}$$

substituting (3.3.5) into (3.3.3), the rate of foreign exchange accumulation becomes

$$\dot{R} = -F(v(e), e) \equiv f(e); \quad f_e > 0 \tag{3.3.6}$$

We assume that a steady state equilibrium exists and there is some $e = \bar{e}$ for which the excess demands for traded and nontraded goods are zero. Our assumption about currency substitution is that the ratio of domestic to foreign currency holdings will be a function of the expected difference of the rates of return of both assets *available* to domestic citizens. In the absence of frictions, and under perfect foresight, this rate of return will equal to the actual percent change in exchange rates, $\dot{E}/E$. However government may effectively impose restrictions on the holding of foreign currencies. These restrictions (*e.g.*, transaction costs) effectively reduce the convenience of holding foreign currency and are modelled here as a tax which reduces the return to holding foreign money. We find it plausible to suppose that the government restrictions depend on the ratio of domestic to foreign real currency holdings. Inverting the demand for foreign currency function we have:

$$\dot{E}/E + t\left(\frac{m}{eR}\right) = L\left(\frac{m}{eR}\right) \qquad (3.3.7)$$

where $L' < 0$, and t is a nondecreasing and possibly non-differentiable function. Taking the logarithmic differential of equation (3.3.1) with equation (3.3.7), some manipulation and μ defined as the nominal money growth rate:

$$\frac{\dot{e}}{e} = L\left(\frac{m}{eR}\right) - t\left(\frac{m}{eR}\right) + \frac{\dot{m}}{m} - \mu \qquad (3.3.8)$$

substituting (3.3.5) into (3.3.4) and rearranging terms yields an expression for m:

$$m = v(e) - eR \qquad (3.3.9)$$

Differentiating totally with respect to time we obtain:

$$\frac{\dot{m}}{m} = \left[\frac{e}{v(e) - eR}\right]\left\{v_e\frac{\dot{e}}{e} - R\frac{\dot{e}}{e} - \dot{R}\right\} \qquad (3.3.10)$$

substituting (3.3.9) and (3.3.10) into (3.3.8) we find our final expression for the changes in the real exchange rate.

$$\dot{e} = \frac{Re^2\lambda}{v - ev_e}\left\{L(\lambda) - t(\lambda) - \mu - \frac{Re^2}{v - ev_e}\right\}$$
$$= J(e, R, \mu, \lambda) \qquad (3.3.11)$$

where $\qquad \lambda = \dfrac{m}{eR}, \quad J_e \gtrless 0, \quad J_R \gtrless 0, \quad J_\mu < 0. \quad (3.3.11')$

The behavior of J is crucial to the analysis. When the exchange control variable t is constant, then constant μ and $L' < 0$ imply the existence of a single locus of points (e, R) such that $\dot{e} = 0$. However, as λ becomes quite small the proportion of domestic real wealth held in foreign money becomes large and the inflation tax base shrinks. As stated before, the control t will be designed to counteract that effect.

To begin, we assume that t is non-decreasing in λ and that as $\lambda \to 0$, $\lambda t(\lambda) \to +\infty$. This will insure an increasing tax or cost of holding foreign balances as the process of substitution away from domestic money continues. Secondly we assume that this occurs fast enough so that below some level of $\lambda = \delta'$, the sign of $\dot{e}$ reverses. Essentially this assumption is that the government will make monetary capital restrictions so tight as to make it unprofitable for domestic residents to increase or maintain their current level of demand for new foreign money.

We can then define two loci of e, R combinations at which $\dot{e} = 0$. First, with little or no capital controls we assume there exists a $\lambda = \delta^*$ such that $L(\delta^*) - t(\delta^*) - \mu = 0$. This may even be a locus where $t = 0$ and non-binding. Second there is the government induced locus described by $L(\delta') - t(\delta') - \mu = 0$. Thus we have a model in which the government may fundamentally change the opportunity cost structure of the two monies through changes in the variable t in a possible non-smooth but regular way.

If the government does not use any of the instruments at its disposal, ($i.e.$, $t = 0$) our model simplifies to that of Calvo and Rodriguez. The equations describing the dynamics of the real exchange rate and foreign currency holding become:

$$\dot{R} = f(e) \tag{3.3.12}$$

$$\dot{e} = J(e, r, \mu) \tag{3.3.13}$$

Figure 1 shows the graphical solution to the system. The schedules $\dot{e} = 0$ and $\dot{R} = 0$ show the combination of e and R which satisfy (3.3.12) and (3.3.13) respectively. The slopes of these are:

$$\frac{de}{dR}\bigg|_{\dot{e}=0} = -\frac{\partial J/\partial R}{\partial J/\partial e} \lessgtr 0; \quad \frac{de}{dR}\bigg|_{\dot{R}=0} = 0$$

Although de/dR is undetermined for brevity we assume $de/dR < 0$ along the $\dot{e} = 0$ locus. The CR analysis showed that the system exhibits saddle-path stability portrayed in Figure 1. The motion of the variables, indicated by the direction of the arrows, is derived from (3.3.12) and (3.3.13).

Following Brock (1974,1975), the usual solution to the potential instability by most writers (*e.g.*, Calvo and Rodriguez (1977)) has been to assume that when no change in exogenous variables is expected, market participants will always choose a path that satisfies the equations of motion and that guarantees path convergence. In short, the problem is eliminated by assuming that the economy immediately moves to the saddle path because rational agents realize that the unstable path cannot be maintained forever. However convergence to a pure foreign currency economy, (*i.e.*, an unstable path to a finite fixed eR and $\lambda = 0$) does not violate this notion of rationality.

Figure 1

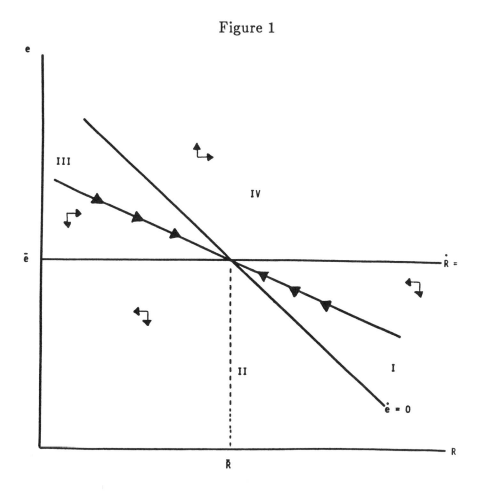

4. EQUILIBRIUM WITH GOVERNMENT INTERVENTION

In this section we analyze the effect of currency controls on the equilibrium paths of the economy. We begin by assuming the growth rate of money, μ, is given. If μ is high relative to foreign currencies it may induce a movement out of the domestic currency, the so-called "dollarization" phenomenon in Latin America. (See Ortiz and Solis (1979).) In this case if the government is to pre-

vent the economy from being completely dollarized and continue
the domestic money creation, it is necessary for the domestic authorities to control the total amount of circulating foreign currency. Given the domestic money creation, control of domestic
holdings of foreign currency is equivalent to controlling the composition of domestic residents' portfolios. Recall that our stock
controls are portfolio transactions costs $t(\lambda)$ which we assumed
were sufficiently strong to induce at a level of $\lambda = \delta'$, $\dot{e} = 0$.

To analyze the dynamics of our model it is useful to consider
Figure 2. This figure differs from the standard saddle path pic-
ture by the presence of the line α and regions V and VI. The line
$\alpha(\delta', \mu)$ is taken to represent the locus of points (e, R) such that
$\dot{e} = 0$ is induced by government restrictions increasing the cost
of holding foreign money balances. Because of our montonicity
assumptions to the right of the line α, $\dot{e} < 0$. That is, the government restrictions reduce the real demand for foreign currency and
therefore reduce its real relative price. However, so long as e is
above $\bar{e}$, foreign assets are sufficiently attractive to induce continued accumulation, albeit at a lower rate. Below the line $e = \bar{e}$ and
above the currency controls line α, both the real exchange rate
and the holdings of foreign money are falling.

In regions V and VI restrictions on ownership of foreign de-

Figure 2

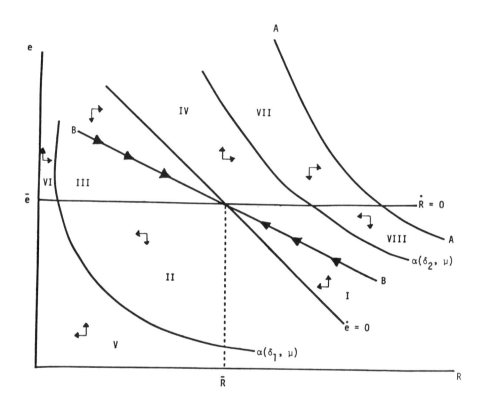

posits (*e.g.*, taxes on foreign balances or outright confiscation of some balances) force the relative price of traded goods down and reduce the foreign component of the money stock. We have hypothesized that regardless of where the economy enters region V, the controls will be harsh enough to force the economy into region VI. Thus, in our small open economy, control of the domestic money stock requires perforce the willingness to impose exchange controls.

Throughout the analysis we will purposely ignore the unstable region below and to the left of the saddle path. This is simply because our focus here is on situations of currency flight which are represented by points above and to the right of the sadlle path. (See Canto and Nickelsburg (1984).) Now, consider an economy beginning on the saddle path BB. Given our assumptions, the economy will move monotonically toward the steady state equilibrium. However, suppose the economy begins at another point. So long as it is above the BB line, there will be increasing real exchange rates and eventually increasing foreign denominated real balances. Therefore any economy starting at a point above BB will eventually find itself in a situation of currency flight.

A description of possible dynamic paths is shown in Figure 3. Of particular interest is the point b. This is the government created equilibrium point and is defined by the choice of μ and δ'. At this point controls exactly offset the market forces and prevent foreign real balances from changing. While it is clearly an unstable equilibrium in the sense of an economy ever "landing" on b except by chance, it does possess a kind of cyclic stability.

To examine point b consider a crossing from region VI to region I above the $\overline{BB}$ line. This will result in a path which di-

Figure 3

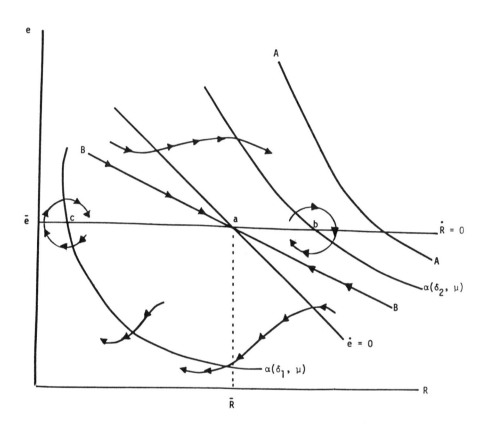

verges from the *laissez faire* equilibrium through region IV. From region IV all paths lead to a decreasing λ until line $\alpha(\delta', \mu)$ is crossed. At this point binding controls increase λ into region VI and ultimately back to region I. Thus, paths about the unstable government equilibrium *b* alternate between regimes of *laissez faire*-exchange arrangements and capital control-exchange arrangements. The cyclic path in Figure 3 about *b* is one which represents the phenomenon of frequent runs on a currency, currency control and currency decontrol, and therefore it is a path which may describe well the experience of many "crisis-prone" currencies. Interestingly, notice that this equilibrium is consistent with a large fraction of money being held in the form of foreign currency.

The path beginning in region III above $\overline{BB}$ is one in which a gradual, perhaps long-term movement away from domestic currency use occurs. As the path moves through region IV, the proportion of domestic money stock in foreign currency increases and the flight away from domestic currency accelerates. As before, controls are ultimately applied and are binding before the domestic currency is driven out of existence. These dynamics have an empirical analog in the history of currencies for which only infrequent controls are applied.

We complete our discussion of dynamics under controls with an experiment. Suppose an unanticipated decrease of μ occurs. Then the *laissez faire* locus $\dot{e} = 0$ and the point a shift to the left. Since $\alpha_\mu > 0$, the α lines also shift to the left. If the economy does *not* instantaneously jump to the new stable saddle-path, an economy initially at rest at point a will now be on an unstable path. Then the initial inflation in domestic non-traded goods will be more rapid than exchange depreciation ($\dot{E}$), foreign exchange earnings will shrink, and the economy moves inexorably towards a crisis. To prevent complete substitution the government imposes limitations on conversion of domestic currency into foreign currency and raises import tariffs, for example. The economy is then at or to the right of $\alpha(\delta', \mu)$, and a cycle about a new point like point b is entered, a cycle of frequent intervention and import retardation. Simple as it may be this experiment is very suggestive of the current reaction of many Latin American countries after they imposed IMF stabilization policies.

Though these dynamics are only illustrative several observations ought to be made. First, the phenomena they describe are empirically plausible. Though we present only an example, the fact that our theory confronts currency crises in a way which unlike "bubble" models might explain recurrent crises is we believe one of its virtues. Secondly, though government controls create new, unstable equilibria, unlike most exchange rate determination models, these controls are a necessary part of policy if governments in small open economies wish to conduct independent monetary policy. The fact that most governments of the kind we purport to model engage in exchange controls lends some tentative credence to this position.

5. DOMINICAN CURRENCY CRISES

For an example of the way in which our framework can provide insight into foreign exchange crisis phenomena we turn to the
case of the Dominican Republic. Our choice of an example was
guided by two considerations. First, the Dominican Republic is
indisputably a small open economy and therefore closely fits some
of the basic model assumptions. Our *a priori* belief was that if
phenomena such as we describe above occur, we ought to observe
it for this economy, since the possibility of a dollar replacement of
the Peso as money is a plausible scenario. Second, based on previous experience we knew the Dominican Republic had experienced
both foreign exchange controls and periods of liberalization.

The one drawback in analyzing this case was a limitation
in data. We collected domestic prices, money stocks, exchange
rates and dollar holdings of domestic residents from the Banco
Central de La Republica Dominicana. One of the key series, dollar
holdings of domestic residents, was constructed from a semi-annual
survey and was available only over the period 1970-1981. With
only twenty two observations to work with, only a *descriptive data
analysis* was possible. Data for the United States were collected
from the *Federal Reserve Bulletin*.

The two relevant measures for our analysis are the real exchange rate, e, and the level of dollar balances held by Dominican citizens. To construct the real exchange rate, the nominal Dollar/Peso rate was taken and divided by the ratio of U.S. to Dominican prices. Our measures of prices were the consumer price indexes of each country.

The historical pattern of (e, R) combinations is displayed in Figure 4. This plot shows three distinct periods during 1970-1981. The first is the period of 1970-1973. For this sub-period the real value of dollar holdings fluctuated between 45 and 65 million dollars while the exchange rate fell from 2.30 to 1.85. The pattern of (e, R) fluctuations indicate no definable cycles. The second sub-period runs from 1974 to mid-1976. This period looks very similar to the earlier one except for a mean shift to 70 million dollars of holdings. The third sub-period, from the end of 1976 through 1981 is distinct from the other two. In this sub-period dollar balances fluctuate a great deal compared to the 70-75 period. Below we present a descriptive explanation of these episodes based on our previous model and the record of monetary policy and controls in the Dominican Republic.

The first sub-period represented on Figure 4 is part of a larger episode of strict foreign deposit ownership laws which began in 1967 after the Civil War and United States intervention. These

Figure 4

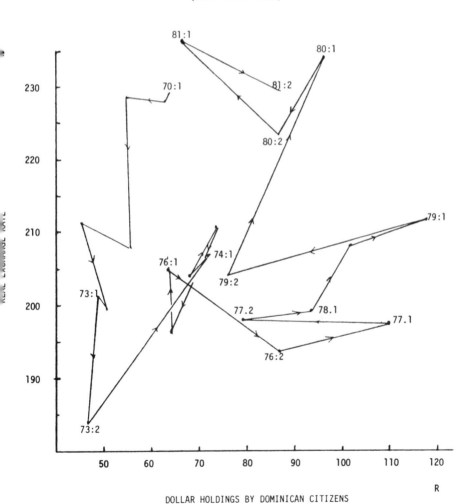

Real Exchange Rates and Real Dollar Holdings
Dominican Republic 1970-1981
(semi-annual data)

DOLLAR HOLDINGS BY DOMINICAN CITIZENS
MILLIONS OF CONSTANT DOLLARS

controls, designed to protect central bank reserves had three major components. First, foreign currency denominated deposits could be held by banks only with a 100% reserve requirement. Secondly, Dominicans were required by law to exchange at par 90% of their foreign exchange earnings. This law essentially and effectively retarded the importation of foreign currencies. Third, import duties were required to be prepaid and import quotas were established. These laws regulated the domestic use of foreign currencies in commodity purchases, and the net effect of the three laws was to drive a wedge between the costliness of exchange with domestic currency and that of foreign currencies. Thus while the real exchange rate responded to underlying real economic conditions and nominal exchange rates reflected real variation as well as relative monetary growth rates, dollar denominated deposits in U.S. Banks remained relatively constant. These deposits, accumulated as an outgrowth of unrepatriated export earnings, were used primarily to finance foreign travel and as security against political instability.

As a result of the 1973 increase in oil prices, the stability of the Domincan Economy appeared weakened. In particular, since the Dominican Republic is not an oil producer we might expect a one time portfolio adjustment out of local currency. The 1973 mean shift from 45 to 70 million dollars in holdings shown in Figure 4 is consistent with this. The dollar ownership restrictions outlined above, remained in force although their form changed from very tight to moderately tight and conversely through this entire episode. Finally we note that during this entire period 1970-1976 gross sugar export earnings, which are taxed to provide government revenue, were either stable or increasing. Consequently government budget deficits and concomitant inflation taxes were moderate. Thus up until 1976 currency restrictions effectively preventing currency flight and dollar holdings were relatively stable, falling slightly on average; both consistent with our theory.

Beginning in 1976 we see a dramatic change in the pattern in Figure 4. The explanation comes from a government decree on July 11, 1976 to end much of the restrictions on ownership of foreign deposits. Beginning with this decree, domestic residents were permitted to legally export non-traditional items in order to obtain foreign currency and to retain the currency. This new policy was instituted to provide incentives for export production, but as a side effect it opened the door to a legal substitution of foreign for domestic currency. Other restrictions such as import quotas and prepayment of duties on many items remained in effect as did restrictions on domestic bank holdings of dollar deposits. Thus while halycon days of free monetary exchange were not ushered in in 1976, a considerable easing took place. This and a gradual increase in the inflation tax due to falling sugar prices were the only significant economic events of the year. Yet it begins a very different episode of currency controls and currency crises, namely one of frequent crises.

Within the 1976-1981 episode there are several turning points in the Figure 4 cycles. According to our theoretical structure these should correspond to changes in currency controls. The first turning point is in the first half of 1977. During 1977, in response to falling sugar prices, increased needs for deficit financing, and the more than doubling of foreign currency owned by domestic residents, the liberalization of the previous year was reversed. The central government increased its control of foreign currency transactions and tightened the import quota requirements. Both measures reduced the rate of return to holding dollars and are reflected in the fall from approximately 100 million dollars to less than 80 million dollars in holdings by the end of 1977. These restrictions lasted less than a year and in early 1978 were relaxed. In the first half of 1979 a new government, facing a currency crises almost identical to the mid-1977 crisis, reinstituted these import controls and tightened further foreign exchange restrictions. These restrictions were severe enough, for example, to terminate the importation of automobiles for a full year. By November of 1979 with the currency crisis well in hand and with a depressed export industry, new export promotion incentive laws were passed. These laws legalized and removed controls on all transactions in dollars which may be related in some way to exports. As a consequence there was once again a flood of new dollars into the Dominican economy seen in the figure as a 20 billion dollar increase in holdings between 79:2 and 80:1. This flow was reversed in late 1980 and early 1981 through letters of credit requirements on selected international transactions, imposed because the Banco Central was experiencing a shortage of foreign exchange. In late 1981, following an initial agreement with the IMF, these restrictions were eased.

6. CONCLUDING REMARKS

We began our anlysis following Chapter 2 with the assumption that in the absence of any official intervention or restrictions, information costs or transaction costs, two fiat monies are identical as assets. The presense of any or all of these market imperfections results in portfolio diversification where at the margin rates of return are equated. To capture this notion empirically we adapted the currency substitution model and demonstrated how government restrictions and interventions create new equilibria which are seemingly stable.

An important aspect of this view of foreign exchange markets is the blurred distinction between fixed and floating exchange rate regimes. In our framework a continuum of government policies and restrictions existed covering the set of regimes from fixed and unchanging exchange rates to freely flexible exchange rates. Much of the existing literature on small developing economy exchange rates then might be recast as particular special cases of an enriched empirical framework built along these lines.

In the following chapters we will examine these implications indirectly. Our empirical work will be guided by the microfoundations of Chapter 2 and the aggregative model of this chapter, but our primary focus will be on describing money demand functions and the relations between domestic and foreign money and monetary phenomena. Our approach there will be primarily statistic.

REFERENCES

Bavesi, G. and P. Grauwe, 1977, Vicious and virtuous circles: a theoretical analysis and a policy proposal for managing exchange rates, *European Economic Review* 10, 277-301.

Bilson, J.F.O., 1979, The 'vicious circle' hypothesis, *IMF Staff Papers* 26, 1-37.

Brock, W.A., 1974, Money and growth: the case of long-run perfect foresight, *International Economic Review* 15, 750-777.

Brock, W.A., 1975, A simple perfect foresight monetary model, *Journal of Monetary Economics* (April), 133-150.

Bruno, M., 1978, Exchange rates, import costs and wage-price dynamics, *Journal of Political Economy* 86, 309-332.

Calvo, G.A, 1983, Staggered contracts and exchange rate policy, mimeo, Columbia University.

Calvo, G.A. and C.A. Rodriguez, 1977, A model of exchange rate determination under currency substitution and rational expectations, *Journal of Political Economy* 85, 617-624.

Canto, V., 1981, A monetary approach to exchange rates with currency substitution: the small open economy case, mimeo, Department of Finance and Business Economics, University of Southern California.

Canto, V. and G. Nickelsburg, 1984a, Currency crises and exchange rate instability in *Dynamic Modelling and Control of National Economies*, T. Basar and L.F. Pau, eds. Pergamon Press: New York.

Canto, V. and G. Nickelsburg, 1984b, Hacia una teoria de tipos de cambio, *Monetarisimo vs. Structuralisimo*, Banco Central de la Republica Dominicana.

Dornbusch, R. and P. Krugman, 1976, Flexible exchange rates in the short run, *BPEA* 7, 537-575.

Fischer, S., 1974, Capital accumulation on the transition path in a monetary optimizing model, *Econometrica* 47 (November), 1433-1439.

Flood, R.P. and P.M. Garber, 1980, Market fundamentals versus price level bubbles: the first tests, *Journal of Political Economy* 88, 745-770.

Flood, R.P. and P.M. Garber, 1981, A systematic banking collapse in a perfect foresight world, Working Paper no. 691, NBER.

Flood, R.P. and P.M. Garber, 1982, Gold monetizations and gold discipline, *Journal of Political Economy* 92, 90-107.

Garber, P.M., 1981, The lender of last resort and the run on the savings and loans, Working Paper no. 823, NBER.

Goldstein, M., 1980, Have flexible exchange rates handicapped macroeconmic policy? Special paper on International Economics no. 14, International Finance Section, Department of Economics, Princeton University.

Kareken, J. and N. Wallace, 1981, On the indeterminacy of equilibrium exchange rates, *Quarterly Journal of Economics* XCVI, 202-222.

Kouri, P., 1976, The exchange rate and the balance of payments in the short run and in the long run: a monetary approach, *Scandinavian Journal of Economics* 78 (May), 280-304.

Krugman, P., 1979, A model of balance-of-payment crisis, *J.M.-C.B.* 11 (August), 311-325.

Lucas, R.E., 1975, An equilibrium model of the business cycle, *Journal of Political Economy* 83 (December), 1113-1144.

Nickelsburg, G., 1984, Flexible exchange rates with uncertain government policy, *Review of Economic Studies* 51, 509-519.

Obstfeld, M., 1982, Relative prices, employment and the exchange rate in an economy with foresight, *Econometrica* 50, 1219-1242.

Obstfeld, M and K. Rogoff, 1982, Speculative hyperinflations in maximizing models: can we rule them out? *Journal of Political Economy* 91, no. 4 (August), 675-687.

Ortiz, G. and L. Solis, 1979, Financial structure and exchange rate experience: Mexico, 1954-1977, *Journal of Development Economics* 6, 515-548.

Salant, S., 1983, The vulnerability of price stabilization schemes to speculative attacks, *Journal of Political Economy* 91, no. 1 (February), 1-37.

Sargent, T.J. and N. Wallace, 1973, The stability of models of money and growth with perfect foresight, *Econometrica* 41, 1043-1048.

Sjaastad, L, 1983, Failure of economic liberalism in the cone of Latin America, *World Economic Affairs* 1, 5-26.

Wenocur, R.D.S. and S. Salant, 1981, Recurrence of a modified random walk and its application to an economic model, *Siam Journal of Applied Mathematics* 40 (February), 163-166.

CHAPTER 4

Currency Substitution and

Small Open Economies:

The Case of the Dominican Republic[1]

The afore cited currency-substitution literature explains the so-called 'dollarization' phenomenon as by shifting individual portfolio balances but fails to explain or account for the degree of government intervention in the foreign exchange market as well as the effect of the government actions in the determination of the level of the exchange rate. As shown in the last two chapters, these omissions are important. The purpose of this chapter is to further develop and to estimate an exchange-rate model that accounts for the 'dollarization' phenomenon as well as domestically imposed transactions costs on the use of the foreign currency.[2]

Following our earlier theory the analysis here views the process of exchange-rate determination as a monetary phenomenon. The model extension is sufficiently general to account for various alternative views. In contrast to the standard monetary approach to exchange-rate determination, our formulation does not explictly assume a preferred habitat view of money demand, whereby the domestic currency is the only medium of exchange used for domestic transactions. Rather, we follow Calvo and Rodriguez (1977), Miles (1978), and Girton and Roper (1981) and our previous theory to develop a model which allows for the possibility of currency switching.

The chapter is organized as follows: Section I discusses some of the institutional arrangements that may exist in a developing nation. More specifically, since the model is estimated using data from the Dominican Republic, this section will stylize the Dominican Republic features. Section II develops the empirical model which determines the currency choice. The effect of monetary policy and of restrictions on the use of the foreign currency in domestic transaction on 'parallel' market exchange rates are established.

In Section III, following the methodology developed by Box and Jenkins (1976), the model is estimated using monthly data spanning the period from June 1969 to March 1979. The estimated coefficients are then used to make inferences about alternative hypotheses. The empirical results are consistent with the implications of the model for the case in which both the elasticity of substitution between domestic and foreign monies and the responsiveness of the transaction costs to exchange-rate levels are large. Section IV presents a summary of the conclusions and policy implications of the paper.

1. STYLIZED INSTITUTIONAL FEATURES OF THE DOMINICAN REPUBLIC PARALLEL MARKET

Since the creation of its Central Bank in 1948, the Domincan Republic has maintained an official one-to-one parity with the US dollar. The initial arrangement was to allow the peso and the dollar to circulate side by side for a few years, until a point at which the Dominican peso would become the legal tender. This period was characterized by the absence of foreign exchange restrictions. The balance of payments, in turn, behaved along the lines suggested by the monetary approach to the balance of payments.

However, since the early 1960s the seigniorage has not been sufficiently large to finance the government budget deficits. As a result, the Dominican monetary authorities have increased the money supply growth at a rate faster than the amount required to maintain external balance. In 1967 after the Civil War and the United States' intervention, the authorities enacted a series of restrictions on foreign deposit ownership in order to protect the Central Bank's reserves.[3] Throughout this period the Dominican monetary authorities pursued a dual exchange-rate system whereby the Central Bank provided foreign exchange at the official parity rate to activities deemed important to the economic development plans of the country. Importation of all other goods and services (as well as private capital flows) were allowed as long as importers provided their own foreign exchange. Largely as a result of this policy, the Dominican Republic simultaneously experienced fluctuations in the black market exchange rate, as well as in the balance of payments. The dual exchange-rate policy resulted in a weakening of the economy's balance of payments adjustment mechanism while simultaneously strengthening the role of the black market as an equilibrating mechanism toward excessive domestic credit creation.

Throughout the period analyzed in this paper, June 1969 to March 1979, the Dominican authorities did not attempt to directly regulate the black market, nor did they alter the official exchange rate.[4] In this regard, the Dominican experience was different from that of the crawling-peg or managed-float exchange-rate system enlisted by many countries during the last decade.[5] Even though, in principle illegal, the black market was allowed to operate freely in order to alleviate the pressures on the Central Bank. Furthermore, the black market was officially renamed the 'parallel market' in order to eliminate the illicit connotation of the old name.

There are several institutional features of the 'parallel market' worth noting. First, since there were no 'official' exchange-rate locations, the market produced its own conveniently located houses of exchange. Secondly, since there were no restrictions to entry, individual transactors could be found in major tourist stops, outside hotels, banks, and in other centrally located places. Third, the exchange price was subject to negotiation and as a result, would differ not only across locations but also across transactions in a given location. Fourth, while the monetary authorities allowed dollar deposits in domestic banks, these funds could not be used to settle domestic transactions. Thus, domestic transactions settled in the foreign currency had to take the form of cash payments or of checks drawn on foreign banks. Also, the Central Bank was able to collect daily information from the major foreign exchange dealers on the average transaction price. Thus, during the 1969-79 period, many of the institutional features of the Dominican Republic resembled closely the ones assumed in the rational expectations literature, such as informationally separated markets, the lack of a forward foreign exchange, and the unweighted market index for the exchange rate.

Beginning in 1979, a new administration instituted import

controls and tightened further the foreign-exchange restrictions. These import prohibitions greatly reduced the government tax revenues; this, combined with the new administration's expenditure and employment programs resulted in record deficits. The monetization of the budget deficits created severe balance of payment problems and as a result, the Dominican Republic Central Bank did not met its international obligations. Largely as a result of the monetization of the deficit during the last couple of years, the exchange rate depreciated at what is considered by Dominican standards an unprecedented rate. In attempts to control the rate of depreciation the authorities have abandoned the previous policy of not directly interfering in the market.[6]

2. THE EMPIRICAL MODEL

The model is characterized by the following equations:

$$p^d = e + p^f \tag{4.2.1}$$

$$E[p^d] - p^d - [E(p^f) - p^f] = Ee - e \tag{4.2.2}$$

$$L^J = aY^J - b(E[p^J] - p^J) \tag{4.2.3}$$

$$L_d^d - L^d = \gamma^d - \phi(1-\alpha)\{(E[p^d] - p^d) - (E[p^f] - p^f) - \tau\} \tag{4.2.4}$$

$$L_f^d - L^d = \gamma^f + \phi\alpha\{(E[p^d] - p^d) - (E[p^f] - p^f) - \tau\} \tag{4.2.5}$$

$$\tau = \mu_1 e - \mu_2 \{ (E[p^d] - p^d) - (E[p^t] - p^t) \} \qquad (4.2.6)$$

$$M^d - p^d = L_d^d \qquad (4.2.7)$$

$$M^f - p^f = sL^f + (1 - s)L_f^d \qquad (4.2.8)$$

$$M^f - p^f = L^f \qquad (4.2.8')$$

where p^d and p^t denotes the logarithm of the domestic and foreign price level, e the logarithm of the parallel market exchange rate, E the expectation operator, L^J the logarithm of country J's demand for real balances, a the income elasticity of demand for real balances, Y^J the logarithm of country J's real income, b the semi-elasticity of demand for real balances, L_f^d, L_d^d the logarithm of the small country derived demand for foreign and domestic real balances, γ_1^f, γ^d as parameter denoting the efficiency of foreign and domestic money in the production of real balances, ϕ the elasticity of substitution between domestic and foreign money, $(1 - \alpha)$ the share of foreign money in the production of real balances, τ the transaction costs on the use of foreign money imposed by the domestic monetary authorities, μ_1 the elasticity of transaction cost to changes in the exchange rate, μ_2 the semi-elasticity of transaction cost due to inflation rate differential across countries, M^f, M^d the logarithm of the nominal stock of foreign and domestic money, s the relative size of the country issuing the international medium.

The economy is characterized as a small open economy. Since we do not allow for the existence of nontraded goods, in absence of any frictions international commodity arbitrage and capital mobility will result in the law of one price (equations (4.2.1) and (4.2.2)).[7]

Recently, Thomas (1985) has shown that the composition of an investor's asset portfolio is independent of his currency holding or the transaction services that the currencies provide. He argues that increases in foreign currency holding could be financed entirely by foreign borrowing. His results show that one can separate the transaction motive from the portfolio motive. He also shows that the concept of currency substitution and of 'dollarization' can only be explained in the context of transaction cost motives. For this reason we assume that currencies reduce frictional losses from transacting in the goods markets (equation (4.2.3)). Within this framework, economic agents hold each currency until the marginal unit of the currency produces transaction services equal in value to its holding costs. For ease of exposition it is assumed that the real income of the rest of the world, as well as that of the small country, are fixed at their full employment levels.

Throughout, the world supply of a given money is assumed to be non-interest-bearing and under the control of the relevant mon-

etary authorities. Two countries are initially assumed; one country's currency is used as the international medium of exchange. In
what follows we assume that residents of the country issuing the
international medium of exchange will have no need to diversify
their currency holding for transaction purposes.

In order to allow for switching among the different monies
by local residents, the demand for real balances is assumed to be
of the CES variety. Equations (4.2.4) and (4.2.5) characterize, in
log-linear form, the derived demand for each of the two currencies.

In order to prevent the displacement of the local currency, the
monetary authorities of the small open economy impose restrictions on the use of foreign currency in domestic transaction. In
addition, the authorities also attempt to regulate the stock as well
as the flow of foreign currency held by domestic residents. Therefore, the government may influence the stock of foreign currency
circulating in the economy through the imposition of restrictions
(e.g., transaction costs) that reduce the convenience of holding
foreign currency. We find it plausible to model such a tax as proportional to the value of the exchange rate in the parallel market.
Similarly, the flow of foreign exchange may be regulated to capital
controls. Equation (4.2.6) represents our attempt to model the
transaction costs imposed by the monetary authorities in order to

prevent the erosion of the inflation tax base.

Worldwide equilibrium requires the equality of the world demand for the two real monies with the world money supply. Equation (4.2.7) reflects the assumption that the small country's currency is held only by its residents. On the other hand, equation (4.2.8) indicates that the world demand for the international
medium of exchange currency depends on the rest of the world demand for that currency as well as the small country's demand for
the foreign currency. That is, the world demand for the international currency is a weighted average of the individual countries'
demands for that currency. To the extent that the open economy in question is small, its effect in the determination of the
equilibrium condition for the international currency may be safely
approximated by the rest of the world demand for that currency
(*i.e.*, $s = 1$). The market clearing condition (equation (4.2.8) may
be approximated by equation (4.2.8′).

Enough relationships have been accumulated by now to allow
one to derive an expression for the derived demand for domestic currency. After substituting the demand for domestic currency (equation (4.2.4) into the market clearing condition (equation (4.2.7)), and the rest of the world demand for dollars into
equation (4.2.8), and after some manipulations, yields the follow-

ing expression for the parallel market exchange rate:

$$e = \frac{-\gamma^d(M^d - M^f) - a(Y^d - Y^f) + [b + (1 - \alpha)\phi(1 + \mu_2)]Ee}{[1_b + (1 - \alpha)\phi(1 + \mu_1 + \mu_2)]}$$

$$(4.2.9)$$

2.1 Solution to the Market Clearing Exchange Rate under Imperfect Information

Prior to considering the formation of expectations, it is first necessary to specify the process generating the growth of the different monies M^f and M^d. In what follows it is posited that M^f and M^d are a function of a constant growth rate (assumed to be zero for simplicity), and of random terms m^f and m^d, respectively. Thus,

$$M_t^d - M_{t-1}^d = m^d \qquad (4.2.10)$$

$$M_t^f - M_{t-1}^f = m^f \qquad (4.2.11)$$

where m^d and m^f are normally distributed white noise processes with zero mean and constant variances σ_d^2 and σ_f^2, respectively.

To model the functioning of the economy under imperfect information, it is a convenient abstraction to think that economic activity in the economy occurs in a continuum of physically and informationally separated market locations. It is assumed that information flows instantaneously across the agents within any location, but it is propagated to the rest of the economy with a one period lag. Under these assumptions, unexploited profits opportu-

nities will not exist when there is only one price for each location.

But, prices may differ across locations. Thus, the expectations op-

erator denotes the current expectations about the current values

of the market clearing prices, domestic and foreign monies which

are available to market participants within one period lag.

The spot exchange rate is viewed here as resulting from the

optimizing behavior of the household under imperfect information.

The formation of expectations is assumed to be rational in the

sense of Muth (1961). Given current available information, par-

ticipants in each market use the structure of the economy, which

is known to everyone, to form the operational forecast of the ex-

change rate. Furthermore, actions based on these forecasts gen-

erate the assumed structure. The equilibrium values of exchange

rates can be shown to be[8]

$$e_t(z) = \frac{(M_{t-1}^d - M_{t-1}^f) - K}{1 + \phi(1 - \alpha)\mu_1} + [m_t^d - m_t^f + \epsilon_t^d(z) - \epsilon_t^f(z)]$$

$$\times \left[\frac{1 + (\theta_1 - \theta_2)[b + (1 - \alpha)\phi(1 + \mu_2)]}{1 + b + (1 - \alpha)\phi(1 + \mu_1 + \mu_2)} \right] \qquad (4.2.12)$$

In turn, an aggregate spot price index, e_t, can be calculated as

a (geometric, unweighted) average of the spot price where the

relative disturbance terms $\epsilon_t^d(z)$ and $\epsilon_t^f(z)$ are averaged out in determining e_t.

$$e_t = \frac{(M_{t-1}^d - M_{t-1}^f) - K}{1 + \phi(1-\alpha)\mu_1} + (m_t^d - m_t^f)$$

$$\times \left[\frac{1 + (\theta_1 - \theta_2)[b + (1-\alpha)\phi(1+\mu_2)]}{1 + b + (1-\alpha)\phi(1+\mu_1+\mu_2)} \right] \qquad (4.2.13)$$

The literature of the monetary approach to exchange-rate determination suggests that fully anticipated changes in domestic money supply will have a proportionate effect in the exchange rate (see Mussa, (1976) and Bilson, (1979)). Similarly, due to imperfect information, this literature suggests that unanticipated changes in domestic money supply will have a positive and less-than-proportionate effect on exchange rates. Upon inspection of equation (4.2.13), it is apparent that these results will be obtained only if the domestic residents choose to hold only the domestic currency irrespective of market conditions (*i.e.*, $\alpha = 1$ and $\phi = 0$). Equation (4.2.13) suggests that the larger are the magnitude of the elasticity of substitution between the two currencies (ϕ) and the responsiveness of transaction costs to the parallel market exchange rate (μ_1), the smaller will be the impact of anticipated money growth in the exchange rate. Similarly, notice that for large values of ϕ and μ_1, the sign of the effect of unanticipated changes in the money supply approaches ($\theta_1 - \theta_2$). Hence, if the foreign money contribution to the exchange-rate variance, θ_2, exceeds that of the domestic money, θ_1, the effect of unanticipated changes in the domestic money supply could be negative. If sufficiently strong, the domestic controls could effectively reduce the domestic currency contribution to the exchange rate. This will be the case if the transactions cost increase the demand for domestic currency by the same amount by which the authorities are increasing the money supply. The assumptions of imperfect information, yields the conclusion that unanticipated money growth results in a less-than-proportionate depreciation of the exchange rate.

The controls affect the relative demand for the two currencies. In principle, if they are sufficiently strong then the controls could be such that they increase the relative demand for pesos by the full amount of the excess money growth. In this case there would be no depreciation of the parallel market exchange rate. On the other hand, if the elasticity of substitution between the two currencies were zero, there would be no substitution between the currencies, and excess monetary growth would result in domestic inflation with a corresponding depreciation of the peso. Hence, in absence of any substitutability between the two currencies, controls will have no effect on exchange-rate determination.

To summarize, the extension of Chapter 3's theoretical model here is sufficiently general to incorporate the possibility that currency substitution is unimportant because the two currencies are not substitutes for each other, and/or because government controls prevent the substitutions from taking place. Interestingly, for the case where the controls do not completely prevent the substitution of the dollar for the peso, our model suggests an excess domestic money supply will lead to a less-than-proportionate depreciation of the peso. Furthermore, if one is willing to accept the view that government-imposed transaction costs exceed 100 per cent of the opportunity cost of holding dollars (*i.e.*, $\mu = 1$), then Dominican citizens would specialize in the use of the peso. Given this assumption one can make inferences about the degree of substitution between the two currencies by examining the coefficient between anticipated money growth and the exchange rate, and between unanticipated money growth and exchange rate.

3. EMPIRICAL ANALYSIS

The model developed in the second section may be estimated using the methodology developed by Box and Jenkins (1976).

The data in this study come from a variety of sources reporting monthly time series estimates from June 1969 to March 1979. The data on the exchange rate, e, and money supply for the

Dominican Republic, DRM1, were made available by the Dominican Republic Central Bank. The data on the US money supply,
USM1, were obtained from the 1981 money stock measures and
liquid assets data published by the *The Federal Reserve.*

3.1 The Univariate ARIMA Models for the Different Variables

There are alternative techniques for developing estimates of
anticipated and unanticipated changes in economic variables. The
approach followed in this paper is to estimate ARIMA models for
the various series. The fitted values are taken to be the anticipated
values for the variables in question and the innovations in the series
are taken to be the unanticipated changes in the series.

The estimated ARIMA models are shown in Table 4.1. The
US money supply appears to be adequately represented by an or-
dinary moving average parameter and a seasonal moving parameter. The Dominican money supply is represented by a seasonal
moving average parameter, and the exchange rate is represented
by a slightly more complicated model, a seasonal autoregressive
parameter and a second order moving average parameter. The
models shown in Table 4.1 perform reasonably well in removing
serial correlations from the respective series. For each equation, no
single autocorrelation exceeded the two standard errors, and the

$Q^*(12)$ is below the 5% critical value under the null hypothesis of no autocorrelations. Additional checks for the model adequacy included 'overfitting' with additional parameters and testing for their exclusion.

3.2 Causal Structure Between the Exchange Rate and Domestic Money Supply

The stylized facts presented in this paper suggest a parallel market where the exchange rate is determined by the demand and supply for foreign exchange by the private sector. This does not suggest that the domestic authorities have had no influence on the equilibrium value of the exchange rate. In fact, the model developed suggests two possible avenues of governmental influence; one is through domestic money creation and the other is through the imposition of transaction costs on the use of the foreign money to prevent an erosion of the inflation tax base. To the extent that the transaction costs are imposed to accommodate the excess domestic money creation, one would still expect a causal relationship going from the money supply to the exchange rate.

An alternative view of the stylized facts for other developing countries is as follows: the foreign exchange market is not really a market in the sense that the price is determined by private supplies and demands. The Central Bank/government sector dominates

Table 4.1: Univariate ARIMA Models for the Different Time Series for the Period Including June 1969 to March 1979.

	Δ_{12} ℓn USM1	$\Delta\Delta_{12}$ ℓn DRM1	$\Delta\Delta$ ℓn e
Constant Term	suppressed	suppressed	suppressed
Moving average parameters			
θ_1	0.172 (0.098)	---	suppressed
θ_2	---	---	0.184 (0.101)
Seasonal moving average parameter			
θ_{12}	0.706 (0.089)	0.884 (0.0447)	---
Seasonal autoregressive parameters			
ϕ_{12}	---	---	-0.742
Q12	8.28	7.53	99.14
d.f.	(10)	(11)	(10)
P-value	0.655	0.767	0.593
Summary statistics			
Adjusted R^2	0.229	0.385	0.190
F	16.6	66.7	13.3
d.f.	(2,103)	(1,104)	(2,103)
Standard error of regression	0.00708	0.0392	0.00921

Note: Standard errors in parenthesis below parameters estimates; Δ denotes the first difference operator $\Delta X_t = X_t - X_{t-1}$; d.f. denotes the degrees of freedom.

that market by its own reserve demand behavior. In effect, it pegs the foreign exchange rate allowing the domestic money stock to respond endogenously. From time to time the government changes the exchange rate (in some cases more or less continuously) in order to achieve a desired path for reserves and other domestic variables. These stylized facts do suggest a causal relationship going from the exchange rate to the money supply.

Evidence in favor of either hypothesis may be obtained by looking at the causal relationship between the Dominican Republic money supply, DRM1, and the exchange rate, e.

While not the only definition of causality, the cross-correlation between the prewhitened residuals of estimated ARIMA models for the money supply and exchange rate reported in Table 4.2 are utilized to examine the causal relationship between the Dominican money supply and the exchange rate. Haugh (1976) has shown that the asymptotic distribution of these cross-correlations under the hypothesis that the innovations are normal and i.i.d. is the same as the asymptotic distribution of cross-correlations of the true innovations of the respective series. In particular, the sample cross-correlations are asymptotically normal and independent across lags with mean zero and variance $(N - |K|)^{-\frac{1}{2}}$ for lag K and N observations. In the data, the coefficient of the cross-correlation between the DRM1 residuals and the e residuals are small for the preceding month and approximately twice their standard deviations for the subsequent month.

Durbin (1970) has shown that the sample cross-correlations of ARIMA residuals at negative lags no longer have the same distribution as would the cross-correlation of true ARIMA innovations, essentially because of dependence between the ARIMA parameter estimates and the cross-correlation estimates. The implication, as pointed out by Pierce (1977), Haugh and Pierce (1977), and Sims (1977) is that the standard error for the negative lag cross-correlation may be less than $(N - |K|)^{-\frac{1}{2}}$. One must therefore be cautious about accepting the hypotheses on the basis of ARIMA cross-correlation of one-way causation from DRM1 to e when the alternative is two-way causation. However, given the basic premise that predictive power, if present, is likely to be strongest at low lags, and that over the sample period e is much more predictable from DRM1 than DRM1 from e, there seems to be a strong case for rejecting the hypotheses of no relation to causality running at least from DRM1 to e. Furthermore, the magnitude of Box-Pierce statistics adjusted for downward bias, S^*, is below its critical values for the twelve leads under the null hypotheses of no autocorrelation with a P-value of 0.442. In short, the cross-correlation

Table 4.2: Cross-correlation Between the Pre-whitened
            Values of e and DRM1

Lead 12	0.053	Concurrent lag	0	-0.201
" 11	-0.106	"	1	0.189
" 10	0.013	"	2	-0.075
" 9	0.040	"	3	0.180
" 8	0.026	"	4	-0.022
" 7	-0.203	"	5	0.057
" 6	-0.023	"	6	0.074
" 5	0.110	"	7	0.193
" 4	0.202	"	8	0.079
" 3	-0.063	"	9	-0.062
" 2	-0.113	"	10	0.145
" 1	0.080	"	11	-0.011
		"	12	0.068
Standard error		0.098		

function suggests a one-way causal relationship going from the money supply to the exchange rate.

3.3 The Transfer Function Model.

The cross-correlation function between the exchange rates and the two money series is the data analysis tool employed here for the identification of the transfer function model.[9] The estimated cross-correlation function suggested that the impulse response function for DRM1 may be adequately represented by two coefficients, a contemporaneous and a one-month lag coefficient. Similarly, the cross-correlation suggests that the impulse response function for USM1 may be adequately represented, at most, by a contemporaneous coefficient.

Two transfer function models are reported in Table 4.3. Upon inspection of the model reported in the first column, it is apparent that the coefficient for the USM1 is imprecisely measured. The second model constrains the USM1 coefficient to be equal to zero.[10] The validity of the restriction imposed in the second model can be tested by examining the ratio of the log likelihood function of the constrained equation to the unconstrained equation.[11] It leads us to accept the second model over the first one. Alternatively stated, no significant relationship between the US money supply and and the Dominican exchange was found. This result is consistent with the currency-substitution hypothesis, which explicitly distinguishes between the US money supply and the world supply of dollars. The currency-substitution model argues that the US money supply is endogenously determined; hence, no systematic relationship is expected. On the other hand the world supply of dollars may be exogenously determined, in which case a negative relationship is predicted. The result does not support the negative relationship predicted by the non-substitution models which equate the USM1 with the world supply of dollars.

The transfer function model reported in the second column yields a number of interesting results. The first one is that the steady state gain is positive and smaller than unity as predicted under the hypothesis that there is currency substitution ($\phi > 0$) and government intervention that attempts to prevent the use of foreign currency in domestic transactions ($\mu_1 > 0$). Another interesting result is that the contemporaneous relationship between the domestic money supply and the exchange rate is negative and significant. Within the context of the theoretical model developed in this paper, this result is plausible under the following conditions: first, that there is a high degree of substitutability between the two currencies; and second, that domestic monetary authorities deliberately alter the transaction costs of using foreign currency on domestic transactions.

The second estimated transfer function model reported in Table 4.3 performs quite well by conventional standards. Diagnostic checks on model adequacy include the Q^* statistic for autocorrelation of residuals as well as the S^* statistic for cross-correlation of residuals suggested by Haugh (1976). None of the individual cross-correlations between residual and forcing variable exceeded

Table 4.3: Transfer Function Model for $\Delta\Delta_{12}$ ℓn e_t

Constant Term	Suppressed	Suppressed
$\Delta\Delta_{12}$ ℓn DRM1		
ω_{10}	-0.0344	-0.0353
	(0.0194)	(0.0193)·
ω_{11}	-0.0611	-0.0625
	(0.0196)	(0.194)
Gain	0.0268	0.0273
	(0.0195)	(0.0144)
S*12		
d.f.	10.6	10.1
	(9)	(10)
P-value	0.409	0.530
ℓn USM1		
ω_{20}	-0.0495	suppressed
	(0.125)	---
Gain	-0.0495	
S*12	8.88	---
d.f.	(9)	---
P-value	0.544	
Noise model		
θ_2	0.281	0.281
	(0.107)	(0.107)
Seasonal autoregressive		
noise parameter		
ϕ	-0.607	-0.589
	(0.125)	(0.122)
Summary statistics		
Adjusted R2	0.277	0.283
F	7.88	9.91
d.f.	(5, 87)	(4, 88)
Standard error		
of regression	0.00920	0.00920
Autocorrelation of residuals		
Q*12	7.8	7.76
d.f.	(10)	(10)
P-value	0.690	0.692

two standard errors and the $S^*(12)$ corresponds to a P-value of 0.530. Also, no single autocorrelation of residual exceeded two standard errors and the $Q^*(12)$ corresponds to a P-value of 0.692.

4. SUMMARY AND CONCLUSIONS

In this chapter monthly data spanning the period from June 1969 to March 1979 were used to study the effects of the US and Dominican Republic money supplies on the Dominican black or 'parallel' market exchange rate. The model was estimated using the methodology developed by Box and Jenkins (1976).

The predictions of the model regarding the sign and magnitude of the different parameters appear to be sustained by the data. Overall, the analytic framework indicated by our analysis is consistent with the hypothesis that excess domestic money creation will induce a dollarization of the economy as well as an exchange-rate depreciation. The results indicate that the contemporaneous relationship between innovations in the Dominican money supply and the exchange rate is negative and significant. The steady-state gain is positive, and significantly smaller than unity.

These two results are supportive of the view that currency substitution is large in the Domincan Republic and that the do-

mestic monetary authorities are aware that the dollarization phenomenon is an attempt to arrest it. They also suggest that as
monetary expansion is planned by the domestic authorities, an
increase in the transaction costs of using the US dollar in domestic transactions will also be planned. This will be implemented
in anticipation of the increase in the domestic money supply and
will thereby induce a shift towards the Dominican peso. To that
extent they are successful, the depreciation of the currency will be
less than proportional to the money supply growth.

Also, the fact that Dominican authorities are not able to completely arrest the dollarization suggests that significant costs would
be incurred in doing so. The negative contemporaneous coefficient
is also easily explained within the model when both the elasticity of substitution and the elasticity of transaction cost with the
exchange rate are fairly large. The fact that our results fail to
uncover any relationship between the US money supply and the
exchange rate is consistent with the currency-substitution hypothesis. This view distinguishes between the world supply of US dollars and the US money supply, as opposed to the nonsubstitution
hypothesis which assumes the two measures of dollar denominated
money to be the same, and as a consequence, predicts a negative
relationship between the US money supply and the exchange rate.

The empirical analysis developed here also sheds some light on two alternative views of the parallel-exchange rate/money supply relationship. The evidence presented in this chapter suggests a causal relationship going from the money supply to the exchange rate rather than the opposite. This evidence clearly supports the hypothesis developed in this paper over the alternative view that the monetary authorities may be pegging the exchange rate while letting the domestic money stock respond endogenously. Due to the structure of the model and the lack of a continuous (monthly) series on dollar holdings of Dominican Republic residents, no direct measure of the elasticity of substitution between the domestic and foreign currency was estimated. However, the estimated coefficients are consistent with a high degree of substitutability. This has profound implications for it suggests that, if unchecked, the dollarization of the economy would greatly diminish the inflation tax base. The data also suggest that the monetary authorities are aware of this and have in effect taken steps to avert the dollarization of the economy by increasing the costs of transacting in dollars. To the extent that a significant amount of resources are devoted by the monetary authorities to arrest the dollarization of the economy, and to the extent that the economy is thus distorted, the net benefits of the inflation tax as a revenue raising measure are greatly diminished. A final implication of our analysis is that a liberalization scheme that reduces the transaction costs of using the foreign currency will lead to a depreciation of the domestic currency.

NOTES

1. This chapter is based on an article entitled "Monetary Policy, Dollarization and Parallel Market Exchange Rates: The Case of the Dominican Republic," *Journal of International Money and Finance* by Victor A. Canto (1985). Duplicated portions reprinted with permission.

2. See Ortiz and Solis (1979) for a discussion of the 'dollarization' of Mexico.

3. The restriction had the following components: First, foreign currency denominated deposits could be held by banks only with a 100 per cent reserve requirement. Second, Dominicans were required by law to exchange at par 90 per cent of their foreign exchange earnings. Third, import duties were required to be prepaid and import quotas were established.

4. Official devaluation requires approval of the Dominican Congress.

5. For an analysis of the monetary approach to the crawling peg, see Blejer and Leiderman (1981).

6. For an explanation and interpretation of the Dominican Republic currency crisis, see Canto and Nickelsburg (1984).

7. The derivation of equation (4.2.2) assumes that either through capital mobility or through trade in goods the real rates are equalized across countries.

8. An appendix with a formal derivation is available from the author upon request.

9. The estimated cross-correlation functions are available from the author upon request.

10. Since the derivation of the equilibrium exchange rate explicitly accounts for the US dollar substitution effects, this characterization of the world demand for US dollars amounts to neglecting the impact rest of the world substitution effects on the US price level. The magnitude of this effect remains an empirical issue. However, since no attempt is made to estimate the effect

of the world supply of dollars on exchange rates, this assumption does not directly affect the empirical analysis performed in this paper.

11. The ratio of the log likelihood function is given by:

$$\lambda = (\sigma_a n / \sigma_0)$$

where σ_0 denotes the standard error of the constrained model and σ_a denotes the standard error of the unconstrained model. Given the nested model λ must lie between zero and unity. The quantity $-2ln\ \lambda$ has a χ^2 distribution in large samples with degrees of freedoms equal to the number of restrictions. One can use the P-value or area under the upper tail of the χ^2 distribution to make inference about the restriction. The high value of λ (*i.e.*, $\lambda = 1$) leads one to accept the second equation as the final model.

REFERENCES

Barro, R., 1976, Rational expectations and the role of monetary policy, *Journal of Monetary Economics* 2 (January), 1-32.

Bilson, J., 1979, Recent developments in the monetary models of exchange rate determination, *International Monetary Fund Staff Papers* 26 (June), 201-223.

Blejer, M., and L. Leiderman, 1981, A monetary approach to the crawling-peg system: theory and evidence, *Journal of Political Economy* 89 (February), 132-151.

Box, G.E.P. and G.M. Jenkins, 1976, *Time Series Analysis: Forecasting and Control*, 2nd ed., Holden Day: San Francisco.

Calvo, G.A. and C.A. Rodriguez, 1977, A model of exchange rate determination under currency substitution and rational expectations, *Journal of Political Economy* 85, 617-624.

Calvo, G., 1983, Lecciones del monetarismo: el cono sud, presented at the 37th Anniversary of the Dominican Republic Central Bank.

Canto, V.A. and G. Nickelsburg, 1984, Towards a theory of currency choice and currency crisis in *Dynamic Modelling and Control of National Economies 1983*, 4th IFACS Conference Proceedings volume, T. Basar and L.F. Pau, eds., Pergamon Press: New York.

Durbin, J., 1970, Testing for serial correlation in least-squares regression when some of the regressors are lagged dependent variables, *Econometrica* 38 (May), 410-421.

Girton, L. and D. Roper, 1981, The theory and implications of currency substitution, *Journal of Money, Credit and Banking* 13 (February), 12-30.

Granger, C., 1969, Investigating causal relations by econometric models and own spectral methods, *Econometrica* 37 (July), 424-428.

Haugh, L., 1976, Checking independence of two covariance stationary time series: a univariate residual cross-correlation approach, *Journal of the American Statistical Association* 71 (June), 378-385.

Haugh, L.D. and D. Pierce, 1977, Causality in the temporal systems: characterizations and a survey, *Journal of Econometrics* 5 (May), 265-294.

Johnson, H.G., 1972, The monetary approach to the balance-of-payments theory in *Further Essays in Monetary Theory*, Allen and Unwin: London.

Johnson, H.G., 1975, The monetary approach to the balance of payments: a nontechnical guide, *Journal of International Economics* 5 (May), 107-151.

Ljung, G. and G. Box, 1976, A modification of the overall χ^2 test for lack of fit in time series models, Technical Report no. 477, Department of Statistics, University of Wisconsin.

Magee, S., 1976, Empirical evidence on the monetary approach to the balance of payments and exchange rates, *American Economic Review* 66 (May), 163-170.

Miles, M., 1978, Currency substitution, flexible exchange rates and monetary independence, *American Economic Review* 68, 428-436.

Miles, M., 1981, Currency substitution: some further results and conclusions, *Southern Economic Journal* 48, 78-86.

Mundell, R.A., 1971, *Monetary Theory: Inflation, Interest and Growth in the World Economy*, Goodyear: Pacific Palisades, California.

Mussa, M., 1976, The exchange rate, the balance of payments and monetary and fiscal policy under a regime of controlled flating, *Scandinavian Journal of Economics* 78, 229-248.

Muth, J., 1961, Rational expectations and the theory of price movements, *Econometrica* 28 (July), 315-335.

Ortiz, G. and L. Solis, 1979, Financial structure and exchange rate experience: Mexico 1954-77, *Journal of Development Economics* 6 (December), 515-548.

Pierce, D.A., 1977, Relationships — and the lack thereof — between economic time series with special reference to money and interest rates *Journal of the American Statistical Association* 72 (March), 11-32.

Salant, S., 1983, The vulnerability of price stabilization schemes to speculative attacks, *Journal of Political Economy* 91 (February), 1-37.

Sims, C.A., 1977, Comment *Journal of the American Statisical Association* 72 (March), 23-24.

Thomas, L.R., 1985, Portfolio theory and currency substitution, *Journal of Money, Credit and Banking* 17, 347-357.

Whitman, M.V.N., 1975, Global monetarism and the monetary approach to the balance of payments, *Brookings Papers of Economic Activity* (3), 491-536.

CHAPTER 5

Dominant Currencies and Monetarism in Argentina

1. INTRODUCTION

The previous chapters have examined directly the question of when currencies are substitutes for each other and how the existence of currency substitution impacts on the ability of policy makers to control domestic inflation and capital flight. In this chapter we examine a set of related questions empirically. Specifically, we ask if the basic underlying propositions of monetary theory are invalidated by the presence of currency substitution or simply masked by the existence of currency substitution. First, the basic propositions of the relationship between the quantity of money and the rate of inflation and exchange depreciation do not seem, at least superficially to hold as a rule. In his well known study of inflation in Latin America Vogel (1974) found past values of money to be significant at the 1% level for only three of sixteen countries. (See his Table 3, p. 108). Secondly, stabilization policy seems to result in increased inflation rates as often as it results in decreased inflation rates. (See Sjaastad (1983) and Calvo

(1984). Thirdly, with very high rates of inflation, and substantially controlled, negative real interest rates, domestic currencies are still being used. For example, in 1984, Argentina had a -200% real interest rate, Peru -40%, and Ecuador -11%. Thus we have a situation where domestic money demand for domestic currency existed only because everyone knew that the government would impose strict controls on foreign money ownership if necessary to retain an inflation tax capability. To examine the above propositions we propose a simple model in which the domestic currency in free markets is an inferior asset, as in the theory of Chapter 3, but in controlled markets is still demanded. We apply our model to Argentina in an attempt to explain some seemingly anomolous stylized facts.

The theory we developed in Chapter 3 when applied to dollarized economies can be viewed as integrating the vehicle currency theories with the currency substitution theories. In the view of the vehicle currency literature, currency choice is determined by transaction cost (see Krugman (1980)). This idea is extended to a currency substitution setting whereby transaction costs influence, and in many instance prevent dollarization (e.g., influence the use of the vehicle currency).

Much of the recent empirical evidence or currency substitution for developed economies seems to indicate an absence of this phenomenon. However, this fact seems curious since the widely observed phenomenon of dollarization in many developing countries (*e.g.*, Ortiz and Solis (1979)) seems to belie the "currency substitution is insignificant" empirical findings reported in the economic literature. However, the dollarization phenomenon suggests a different view of currency substitution; that of a dominant international currency and a domestic currency. That is, we do not observe "cruzadization" or "intiazation" in Argentina, nor "australization" in Brazil or Peru, but we do observe dollarization in all three countries. The notion of currency substitution between any given two currencies, viewing the currency area as incorporating several countries and currencies simultaneously, does not seem to have much empirical validity with respect to developing countries. Yet, this is the phenomenon commonly investigated in the literature (see McKinnon (1982)). Our analysis takes the position that there is currency substitution between the domestic currency and some foreign dominant currency (vehicle currency) which is in perfectly elastic supply at given foreign price levels.

In an environment such as we have described in Chapter 3, the idea of currency substitution as a portfolio choice among several currencies is not valid. Specifically, we are not contemplating a situation where Argentinians and Chileans are deciding jointly of whether or not to use the austral or peso as their currency. Rather, there is an absolute preference for a dominant currency such as the US dollar and the direction of substitution is strictly one-way. Thus, given the costs of holding foreign money imposed by the domestic government, domestic residents will hold the maximum amount of the currency they can afford.

Therefore, during periods of currency liberalization we find rational explosive paths of nominal quantities. These lead ultimately to a currency crisis when the velocity of money is increasing rapidly and the government's ability to finance deficits through money growth is diminishing rapidly. The government then imposes restrictions or costs on ownership of foreign money and recaptures a demand for domestic currency. Since this endemic instability would dominate in any statistical analysis which incorporated a period of liberalization, it would not then be surprising if many of the well known propositions of monetary theory were seemingly unfulfilled.

The two basic propositions we consider are the proposition that price inflation is substantially explained by money growth and the proposition that nominal exchange rate devaluation can be explained by relative money growth. In addition, we examine the independence of real exchange rates from the growth rate of the money supply. For this investigation we study the post-war experience of Argentina which includes several periods of liberalization and several of exchange and currency controls. We find that when one controls for the unstable paths during periods of liberalization, the monetary propositions reappear as empirical regularities.

In the next section we set out our basic empirical model and describe its implications. We then describe briefly the monetary history of Argentina and present some evidence on our propositions. This is followed by a discussion and some results on currency substitution and on money, prices, and exchange rates.

2. BASIC DOMINANT CURRENCY MODELLING CONSIDERATIONS

In this section we modify the model set out in Chapter 3 to be an empirically implementable model. We begin by re-defining what for us is a key variable, λ — the ratio of domestic money real balances to foreign money real balances held by domestic residents. The variable λ thus represents the extent to which domestic residents have been able to substitute out of their own currency. Secondly, we assume that there exists a single foreign money that domestic residents desire, the dollar, and that this currency has

the property that its rate of return net of risk premium is higher
than the domestic rate of return in all future states of the world.
Moreover, since the domestic capital market is heavily controlled
by the government and only partially linked to the world capital
market, foreign real interest rates on risk free securities will dominate domestic securities of similar quality. Therefore, given free
portfolio choice domestic residents will choose to use the foreign
currency and invest in foreign capital markets. We also assume
that the domestic government will permit neither the complete
collapse of its currency nor its .capital markets and therefore sep-
arates the domestic financial economy partially from the foreign
financial world.

To capture these notions, assume that $f_i(\lambda)$ is an exponentially declining function of λ. Thus, when domestic real balances
are becoming a small fraction of real balances, f_i is increasing exponentially. Also, we will abstract here from the role of capital
markets. We then represent money demand as:

$$\pi_t = f_1(\lambda_t) + m_t + \epsilon_{1t} \qquad (5.2.1)$$

where π is the rate of inflation, m the rate of growth of the domestic money stock, and ϵ_1 a random white noise component which
includes supply shocks. In equation (5.2.1) inflation may be driven

by increases in the quantity of money or by increases in the velocity of money f_1. When λ is held more or less constant, equation
(5.2.1) becomes the usual Cagan, log-linear money demand function.

Secondly, we assume that the nominal exchange rate is driven
by capital flight as well as differential rates of inflation. Since
capital markets are controlled in the domestic economy, we do not
place the interest differential as an argument in these functions.
We then have:

$$\dot{E}_t = f_2(\lambda_t) + a_2(\pi_t - \pi_{ft}) + \epsilon_{2t}, \qquad (5.2.2)$$

where $\dot{E}_t$ is the rate of change of the nominal exchange rate, π_{ft}
is the foreign rate of inflation and ϵ_{2t} is a shock to exchange rate
changes. When λ_t is stabilized, the exchange will reflect different
purchasing powers of the two monies through the current account.
The term ϵ_2 could reflect changes in tastes with respect to nontraded goods or changes in the terms of trade.

The terms of trade are assumed to be white noise about a
mean except when currency flight forces them to increase as domestic residents bid up the relative price of foreign goods in an
attempt to rid themselves of domestic currency. Thus, we assume:

$$e_t = f_3(\lambda_t) + \epsilon_{3t} \qquad (5.2.3)$$

where ϵ_3 represents the usual real shock term and e is the rate of change of the terms of trade. Finally, we need to specify a theory of change of λ. We presume that λ has several components. First, the larger is domestic inflation relative to foreign inflation, the larger will be the rate of currency flight. Second, even if domestic and foreign inflation rates are not too different, we assume that when domestic residents are holding large dollar balances, they will try to increase their holdings more rapidly. This assumption is related to the notion of speculative fever in that it attempts to capture the way in which a currency flight tends to feed on itself and build very rapidly. Finally, we posit the existence of government taxes on foreign balances which can halt or even reverse the flight of capital. These can take the form of direct taxes on foreign denominated balances, official conversion rates, confiscation of foreign balances, or other methods of freezing the use of foreign currency in the domestic economy. Some of these methods wil be described later for the experience of Argentina. Our equation for the evolution of real balances is:

$$\dot{\lambda}_t = a_4 - f_4(\lambda_t) + b_4(\pi_t - \pi_{ft}) + \tau(\lambda_t) \qquad (5.2.4)$$

The function τ is our government control function. It is an exponentially declining function of λ constructed by the government in such a way as to close off capital flight, when λ becomes

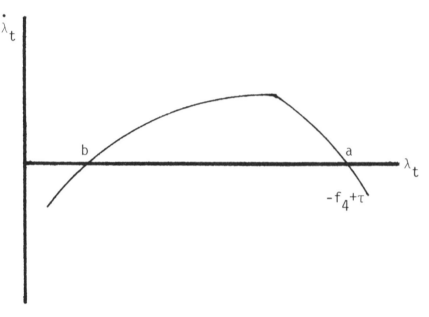

Figure 5.1

small. Ignoring the effects of a_4 and the inflation differential, we can represent graphically the effect of τ on the rate of change of λ by Figure 5.1. The point a represents a *laissez-faire* equilibrium, one which we claim is unstable, and point b the equilibrium with controls on the flow of currency. If τ is applied discontinuously with a large negative jump at point b, then it is possible for controls on currency conversion to decrease the level of foreign real balances. The government may then contemplate a freeing of the controls at a future date. This is certainly a typical pattern for countries which tend to impose currency controls.

The implications of our model are straightforward. When the currency controls τ are non-binding; λ, the nominal and real exchange rates, and the price level should follow explosive paths.

When τ is binding the economy is largely closed with respect to domestic monetary phenomena, and prices and exchange rates should satisfy the usual monetarist propositions. Moreover, even when the economy is following an explosive path, there is an underlying component relating the rate of change of prices to the rate of growth of the money stock and the nominal exchange rate to monetary growth. However, one should not mistake this model for a portfolio choice model. In our model, optimizing agents are forced to choose corner solutions where the constraints are government imposed and therefore the usual interest and rate of return arbitrage conditions do not apply.

When the ratio of domestic money real balances to foreign money real balances are constant, possibly infinite, then the model reduces to a standard simple monetarist model. However, when there are no currency restrictions, the explosive terms represented by the f_i functions are a factor in the model. Thus the empirical challenge is two-fold. First, to examine the basic monetarist propositions in this model for episodes of currency substitution and currency flight and second, to identify the existence of currency flight with our model.

First, we take up the issue of identifying currency substitution. Most previous studies, *e.g.*, Bordo and Choudhri (1982),

Cuddington (1984), and Brittain (1981) examine currency substitution through its portfolio implications for causality and covariation of such variables as velocity across countries. From our point of view, however, these approaches are invalid precisly because they fail to examine the domestic currency choice process directly and this process involves a corner solution for domestic residents. Therefore, we examine the determination of λ directly. For periods when currency controls existed ($\tau(\lambda)$ was binding), we do not expect to find evidence to currency substitution. For evidence on the existence of binding controls see de Macedo (1982, 1983). For periods when some substitution is permitted, we expect to find E_t and λ_t highly correlated. To be precise, if we take equation (5.2.2) and substitute it into equation (5.2.4) we have, with equation (5.2.1):

$$\dot{\lambda}_t = C_4(\lambda_t) + b_4 \dot{m} t - b_4 \pi_{ft} + b_4 \epsilon_{1t} \qquad (5.2.5)$$

If we have assumed controls to be binding, with our assumption that the foreign currency is a dominant asset, (5.2.5) will simply reflect how the built-up pressure on the process of conversion from domestic into foreign currency is alleviated through shifting the C_4 function. In other words, when controls are binding $\dot{\lambda}$ is a policy variable and (5.2.5) describes the policy mechanism C_4. C_4

could be either negative, positive or costant, depending on λ_t. In equation (5.2.5), it is inappropriate to solve for λ_t by integrating forward in time, since it is not future expectations but present legal restrictions which is driving λ_t. Therefore, with appropriate restrictions on ϵ_{1t} and C_4 we may take λ_t to be predetermined.

With λ_t predetemined and the path m_t and π_{ft} exogenous, our exchange rate equation reduces to:

$$\dot{E}_t = C_1 + C_2 \dot{\lambda}_t + V_t \qquad (5.2.6)$$

when v_t is a random shock term incorporating ϵ_{1t}, and ϵ_{ft}. Equation (5.2.6) is in the form of a currency demand equation where C_2 can be interpreted as an elasticity of substitution parameter.

When the stringent assumption of predeterminateness is not met, as will be usual, then there is a simultaneous determination of π_t, e_t, E_t and λ_t. It is therefore very difficult to capture the substitution process in general, though for specific institutional structures and utility functions it will be possible. For our purposes here, however, we note that the model (5.2.1)-(5.2.4) can be written as:

$$\dot{E}_t - f_2(\lambda_t) = a_2(\pi_t - \pi_{ft}) + \epsilon_{2t}$$

$$\dot{e}_t - f_3(\lambda_t) = \epsilon_{3t} \qquad (5.2.7)$$

$$\pi_t - f_1(\lambda_t) = m_t + \epsilon_{1t}.$$

Since our previous theory predicts that during times of freely exchangeable currencies λ_t will be exponentially declining, our hypotheses about the f_i's implies that net of an exponential or explosive trend, our data should reflect the standard dichotomy, neutrality and purchasing power parity assumptions.

We therefore have a methodology for analyzing in a very general sense our postulates about currency substitution. Namely, for periods when it is apparent that agents can rapidly move into the dominant currency the data should be dominated by exponential trends. Therefore, the usual postulates of monetary theory should be obscured in the data and in subsequent statistical analysis. However, when the exponential trends are controlled for, these postulates should reappear in the form of statistically significant parameters.

3. A Summary of Argentina's Exchange Rate Systems 1956-82

We have chosen to apply our model to the experience of Argentina during the post-World War II period because traditionally Argentina has been a high inflation, high government deficit country. Thus, the notion that the government may have to protect its inflation tax base has some credence. Secondly, Argentina has had several periods of liberalization of foreign exchange markets followed by currency crises and currency controls (see Table 5.1). This pattern is also consistent with the kinds of environments we are modelling. Finally, while small country assumptions are probably not warranted in the case of Argentina, the casual evidence suggests a one-way currency substitution process. That is, Argentinians wish to hold the key currency, US dollars while at the same time others do not wish to hold Argentinian pesos. Whenever this occurs, we claim that the portfolio choice for Argentinians is a corner solution, *i.e.*, to purchase as many dollars as is possible given the governmental constraints, actual and implicit, on their actions.

The basic regime structure seems to alternate between relative *laissez-faire* regimes where domestic residents can liquidate assets and convert them to foreign currency balances, trade-only *laissez-faire* which is also characterized by a floating rates system but in conjunction with currency restrictions and tight control regimes with all international transactions requiring pre-approval of the government.

The first part of our data covers the *a foro* system of exchange rates. This was a controls system where all goods were given subjective government values and an equal quantity of for-

Table 5.1: Argentina's Exchange Rate Systems 1956-1982

Period	System
Nov. 1955 to Dec. 1958	A foro (Multiple Exchange Rate)
Jan. 1959 to Mar. 1965	Floating Rate
Apr. 1965 to Early 1971	Fixed Rate
1971 to Dec. 1979	Dual Exchange Rate (Financial Rate Freely Floating)
Dec. 1979 to June 1981	Tablita (Preannounced Rate of Exchange Depreciation)

eign exchange was required to be surrendered after their exportation. Since holdings of foreign exchange were prohibited, this system was one in which currency substitution was unlikely.

In January of 1959, a liberalization of international transactions took place. Although the economy, and in particular capital markets, remained heavily controlled, transactions took place at free market exchange rates. Therefore, it was possible to repatriate dollars and to avoid surrender of the balances to the government. Secondly, there was official encouragement of dollar generating exports. The system of differential and distortionary tariffs was maintained throughout the 1959-1965 period, but it was clearly possible to acquire foreign currency for domestic use.

March 1964 marked the beginning of a series of currency crises. The flow into dollars became a full currency flight and throughout the year measures were attempted to stem attacks on the peso. By March of 1965, it was clear that a regime change would be necessary and a quasi-fixed rate system was imposed. This system was characterized by gradual devaluations in order to maintain external balance, official intervention to maintain the official exchange rate, and a series of tightened controls to maintain the system.

A classic speculative attack on the Central Bank's reserves occurred in September of 1971, and the government introduced a dual exchange rate system. What is important for our purposes is that this system set up a completely unfettered speculative foreign exchange market. Thus once again currency substitution was free to flourish and there began a movement out of Argentinian pesos. The system reached a crisis stage in December of 1979, and the government, no longer able to maintain an orderly domestic currency market in which to finance its deficits, terminated the dual system. Over the next year the government followed a plan of pre-announced mini-devaluations or a *tablita* system. This system was once again one in which international transactions were controlled however with a declining degree of success.

4. THE CASE OF ARGENTINA

To verify that some of the anomalous phenomena we are attempting to explain are present in the Argentinian case we conducted a preliminary econometric examination. Using price, nominal exchange rates, and quantity of money data from the annual report of the Central Bank, and the US CPI price index we estimated price, nominal and real exchange rate equations corresponding to the strict monetarist versions of (5.2.1), (5.2.2) and (5.2.3). The money supply was taken to be the usual M1 concept; the price index is consumer prices for urban families; and the nominal exchange rate is either a free market rate, or when controls existed, a non-preferential official exchange rate.

4.1 Nominal Exchange Rate, Domestic Money Supply Growth and Foreign Prices

The nominal exchange rate regressions are presented in Table 5.2. There are three regressions, two of which correspond to floating rate periods for the years 1959-1965 and 1971-1979. The third regression encompasses the entire sample period (1959-1982). Each equation was estimated with an autoregressive structure for the error terms. From our theory, present and past money sup-

Table 5.2: Exchange Rates and Money Supplies, Argentina 1959–1980, Nominal Values Monthly Data

Dependent Variable = $\Delta E_t/E_t$

Period	Constant	$\Delta M_t/M_t$	$\Delta M_{t-1}/M_{t-1}$	$\Delta P_{us,t}/P_{us,t}$
1959.01–1965.02	0.028 (2.425)	-0.386 (1.200)	-0.080 (0.283)	-4.172 (4.259)
$\bar{R}^2 = .05$	F(4,69) = .98		DW = 1.97	
1971.09–1979.12	.066 (1.793)	-.064 (.324)	.248 (1.236)	2.484 (.696)
$\bar{R}^2 = .25$	F(5,95) = 5.37		DW = 1.88	
1959.01–1980.12	0.016 (1.761)	0.063 (0.0572)	0.168 (1.516)	0.559 (0.398)
$\bar{R}^2 = .14$	F(4,259) = 10.61		DW = 1.90	

Note: Figures in parentheses are t statistics. All series have been filtered to remove autoregressive errors simultaneously with the estimation.

plies and the US price level are exogenous to the nominal exchange rate and should explain most of the exchange rate variation. The results here are quite striking. Although the US price level is a significant explanatory variable for the floating rate period of 1959-1965, the Argentinian money supply is not significant in any of the equations. Thus the usual presumption that changes in the quantity of money and of the foreign price level are the most important variables in predicting nominal exchange rates does not seem to hold here.

4.2 Inflation and Money Supply Growth.

Next, consider the price equations in Table 5.3. When the rate of inflation over the entire 1959-1980 sample is projected on current and past money supplies there is a relatively strong positive correlation. However, the sum of the present and lagged coefficients are .22 and there is a strong first order autocorrelation component. Moreover, less than a third of the variation in the rate of inflation is explained by the quantity of money. To be sure, more sophisticated econometric analysis might reveal a stronger relationship, however, our results do not provide conclusive evidence for the monetarist hypothesis. When we explore further by examining the sub-period 1971-1979, where floating rates and weak currency controls (*i.e.*, a dual exchange rate) prevailed, we

Table 5.3: Inflation and Money Growth, Argentina 1959-1980, Monthly Data

Dependent Variable = $\Delta P_t/P_t$

Period	Constant	$\Delta M_t/M_t$	$\Delta M_{t-1}/M_{t-1}$	ρ
1959.01-1965.02	.0199 (3.193)	.376 (5.785)	.164 (2.570)	.481 (8.228)
$\bar{R}^2 = .46$	$F(4,257) = 75.1$		$DW = 2.006$	
1971.09-1979.12	0.50 (3.48)	.171 (1.770)	0.96 (0.992)	.582 (6.635)
$\bar{R}^2 = .42$	$F(3,95) = 23.29$		$DW = 1.85$	
1959.01-1980.12	.015 (2.838)	.531 (4.341)	-.310 (2.560)	.400 (3.641)
$\bar{R}^2 = .28$	$F(4,67) = 9.86$		$DW = 2.253$	

Note: Figures in parentheses are t statistics. ρ is the first order autocorrelation coefficient.

find that the significant relation between changes in the quantity of money and the inflation rate disappear. Thus, though the proportionate relation between money and prices may hold over some of our sample, it clearly does not for other parts of the sample.

4.3 Real Exchange Rates, Domestic Money Supply Growth and Foreign Prices

We now turn to the real exchange rate. This quantity was calculated by adjusting changes in the nominal rate for changes in the relative ratio of inflation. Therefore our real exchange rate is a constant dollar concept of terms of trade. Recall that our proposition was that in the absence of currency flight, the terms of trade will follow a random walk process, *i.e.*, changes in the quantity of money should not induce real exchange rate effects. For the floating rate periods of 1959-1965 and 1971-1979, two periods of suspected currency substitution, we regressed the real exchange rate on changes in the domestic quantity of money and foreign price levels. For both periods an $AR(2)$ error structure was found to be appropriate. As reported in Table 5.4 neither equation explained very much of the variation of the real exchange rate. Furthermore a 10% level of significance would be required to say that there was explanatory power in these equations. However, both equations show changes in the quantity of money being significant explana-

Table 5.4: Real Exchange Rates and Money Stocks, Argentina 1959-1979, Monthly Data

Dependent Variable = $\Delta e_t/e_t$

Period	Constant	$\Delta M_t/M_t$	$\Delta P_{us,t}/P_{us,t}$
1959.01-1965.02	.017 (1.455)	-.606 (1.859)	-3.961 (0.811)
	$\bar{R}^2 = .05$	$F(5,66) = .93$	DW = 1.87
1979.09-1979.12	.022 (0.957)	-.323 (1.952)	-.349 (0.129)
	$\bar{R}^2 = .20$	$F(5,95) = 5.84$	DW = 1.97
1959.01-1980.12	.001 (0.883)	-.274 (2.72)	.560 (0.431)
	$\bar{R}^2 = .10$	$F(5,259) = 7.9$	DW = 2.009

Note: Figures in parentheses are t statistics. Both equations were estimated with AR(2) error structures.

tory variables for changes in the real exchange rate. Thus, there is a bit of evidence that these two variables are related during the periods under question.

Before turning to our empirical explanation of these apparent anomolous results it is useful to keep in mind some of the monetary history of Argentina during these periods.

The discussion on the Argentinian exchange rate systems suggests an economy in which inflationary finance is being used but in which domestic residents would prefer not to hold domestic money. The government, through its control of various financial institutions, is continually fighting a battle to maintain the ability to tax through the emission of new money. The two major episodes in which floating rates prevailed, 1959-1965 and 1971-1979, should according to our theory be characterized by explosive trends and an absence of the usual relationships between the quantity of money, prices, nominal exchange rates and real exchange rates. As our previous Tables 5.2-5.4 indicate, it is precisely these periods when the traditional postulates of monetary theory appear the weakest.

5. EVIDENCE OF ONE WAY CURRENCY SUBSTITUTION

In the preceding we isolated several periods of the post-war epoch in which the potential for unconstrained substitution out of the Argentine peso into the US dollar could occur. For these episodes our theory suggests that the nonlinear relationship between λ, E and τ would preclude a direct test of the currency substitution hypothesis. Indeed, were these episodes included in an empirical analysis of currency substitution, the simultaneity bias may well give very misleading results. For the other episodes we can employ a direct test of the kind suggested in section 2 since the substitution itself is controlled and recursive. In this section, we present an analysis of the three non-explosive episodes.

In each of these episodes the *a foro* or multiple exchange rate 1956-1959; the fixed rate, 1965-1971; and the *tablita* system, 1979-1980, there was a mixture of pegging the exchange rate through exchange market intervention and controls on currency ownership. For each we can take the contemporaneous level of λ_t, which was dependent upon past monetary behavior, as causally prior to the change in E_t since λ_t reflects the ability to circumvent the various currency restrictions. In other words, because dollars dominate pesos, domestic residents would like to acquire dollars. The fact that λ_t is non-zero reflects the fact that it is not possible to substitute completely away from the domestic currency due to active currency controls and the knowledge that the government prob-

Table 5.5: Elasticity of Substitution Estimates

Period	Constant	$\Delta E_t/E_t$	$\bar{R}^2$	F
1956.01– 1959.02	-.007 (.29)	.516 (1.65)	.05	2.72
1965.04– 1971.08	-.0139 (.579)	.470 (.857)	.01	1.77
1979.12– 1980.12	-.066 (3.3)	1.04 (5.02)	.29	21.10

Note: Montly data. Figures in parentheses are t
statistics.

ably would impose heavy taxes on dollar balances in the event

of a major dollarization of the local economy. Therefore, current

and future monetary policy will not effect λ_t unless it makes the

peso more attractive and undominated by the dollar. Since we as-

sume this is not the case, we take λ_t to be exogenous with respect

to $\Delta E_t/E_t$ and therefore, $\Delta E_t/E_t$ is predetermined relative to

$\Delta\lambda_t/\lambda_t$. Using the previously developed relationships then we can

measure the elasticity of substitution between the two monies by

projecting the growth rate of λ_t on the growth rate of E_t. These

results are presented in Table 5.5.

The first thing to notice about these regressions is that two

of the periods; the floating rate, 1956-1959, and the *tablita*, 1979-

1980; show at least a marginally significant elasticity of substitution. The third period does not; however, this is perhaps not surprising as the government was committing its entire stock of international reserves to guarantee the price of the peso in the wake of the disastrous speculations of 1964 and 1965.

While the results in Table 5.5 are not strong and must be interpreted with a great deal of care, they indicate several important aspects of currency substitution. First, in these three cases the only striking difference in regime structure with respect to holding money is between the *a foro* and *tablita* on the one hand and the mini-devaluation regime of 1965-1971 on the other. The *a foro* and *tablita* systems did not guarantee, even implicitly, future values of the peso by the government. The mini-devaluation system of 1965 to 1971 did provide such a guarantee, For the *a foro* and *tablita* systems, the government believed the system would be self sustaining. Since the history of exchange rate systems belies such confidence it is not surprising that we find substitution occurring here. In the mini-devaluation system, the explanation for a lack of currency substitution is not a belief by domestic residents that the system would hold together forever, but a belief that when it began to fail the government would for a time prop the system up. In this case, there would be no reason to incur the cost of holding dollars currently since they are identical in value to the pesos as long as the system holds together.

Secondly, the elasticity of substitution is higher in the later period than in the earlier ones. While this may simply reflect differentially stronger controls, it may also reflect a learning process and increasing sophistication in avoiding the inflation tax. Finally, because the coefficient estimates and structure seems to be different in these three periods, more carefully detailed models of the interactions of controls with substitution toward a dominant currency is needed.

6. MONEY, EXCHANGE RATES, AND PRICES

In our earlier sections we characterized the two periods, 1959-1965 and 1971-1979, as being episodes during which time unfettered substitution out of the domestic currency could occur. In this section we explore this idea further by showing that in these periods one can provide empirical evidence for our model. This can be done by examining the residual processes for the data once the explosive trends are removed.

We first examine the relationship between the rate of inflation and the quantity of money which in section 5.5 was virtually nonexistent for our two periods. The regressions controlling for the explosive growth of P_t due to the rapidly increasing velocity of money are given in Table 5.6. What is important to notice here is that even though the quantity of money does not enter as strongly here as one might expect from a more sophisticated approach, it clearly becomes a significant explanatory variable for all periods. Thus, one of our puzzles from section 5 has at least a partial explanation.

Secondly, we present the projections of the real exchange rate on the quantity of money in Table 5.7. Recall from Table 5.3 that the growth rate of quantity of money was a significant explanatory variable during these two episodes. As is seen from the table, controlling for the explosive trends removes the indirect influence that the money stock had on the real exchange rates variation, and as would be expected from our model, real exchange rates do not vary significantly with nominal variables. The explanation for the significant relation found before came from the fact that the quantity of nominal balances is related to the rate of inflation and therefore indirectly to the explosive path of λ. Thus, although we did not statistically observe the intermediate linkage in our regression analysis the feedback was sufficiently strong to pick up a significant relation to real exchange rates. It should be noted, however, that a money to real exchange rate influence is

Table 5.6: Inflation and Money Growth, Argentina 1956-1980, Modified Data

Dependent Variable = $\Delta P_t/P_t$

Period	Constant	$\Delta M_t/M_t$	$\Delta M_{t-1}/M_{t-1}$	λ_t
1959.01-1965.02	0.018 (1.616)	-.531 (4.297)	-0.329 (2.702)	0.00 (0.320)
$\bar{R}^2 = .33$	$F(4,93) = 8.2$		$DW = 2.32$	
1971.09-1979.12	.005 (0.314)	.198 (2.161)	.085 (0.930)	.0002 (3.747)
$\bar{R}^2 = .48$	$F(4,91) = 20.6$		$DW = 1.92$	
1956.01-1980.12	0.1356 (1.873)	0.190 (6.713)	0.00 (3.047)	0.427 (0.342)
$\bar{R}^2 = .36$	$F(4,291) = 41.7$		$DW = 2.05$	

Note: Figures in parentheses are t statistics. Data are modified to remove explosive trends during periods of uncontrolled substitution.

Table 5.7: Real Exchange Rates Money Stocks, Argentina 1959-1979, Modified Data

Dependent Variable = $\Delta e_t/e_t$

Period	Constant	$\Delta M_t/M_t$	$\Delta P_{us,t}/P_{us,t}$	λ_t
1959.01-1965.02	0.034 (1.628)	0.553 (1.609)	-2.382 (0.513)	0.00 (1.274)
	$\bar{R}^2 = .08$	$F(5,69) = 1.39$	$DW = 2.06$	
1971.09-1979.12	.030 (0.606)	0.427 (1.720)	1.977 (0.496)	.0001 (0.900)
	$\bar{R}^2 = .09$	$F(5,94) = 2.2$	$DW = 1.87$	
1959.01-1980.12	.004 (.214)	-.309 (2.395)	-.191 (.106)	0.00 (.295)
	$\bar{R}^2 = .04$	$F(5,256) = 2.98$	$DW = 1.89$	

Note: Figures in parentheses are t statistics. Data are modified to remove explosive trends during periods of uncontrolled substitution.

still present, although weaker in the 1959 to 1980 regression.

Finally, we examine the seeming independence of nominal exchange rates and the domestic money supply. Unfortunately, over the entire unstable period the results of Table 5.2 seemed to hold even when explosive paths were controlled for. The explanation for this seems to lie in the fact that the nominal exchange rate was not free to reflect market, and in particular trade in commodity, pressures. For example, the monetary authorities in anticipation of increased money supply growth probably increased the restrictions on the use of foreign currency. This in turn increases the demand for local currency which reduces the pressures for the exchange rate to depreciate. Thus, as part of the attempt of the government to control currency flight, frequent interventions and rule changes are deserved.

We estimated the relationship between changes in the quantity of money and nominal exchange rates for a subperiod of the mid 1970's floating rate regime. It should be noted that this is the only subperiod for which we found the following results. Table 5.8 presents the regressions both with and without controlling for the explosive path. The regression of nominal exchange rates on money without controlling for currency flight is similar to those in Table 5.2, namely there is no significant money supply effect.

When we modify the data to remove exponential trends however, we do pick up a significant money supply effect as we would expect from our theory.

Table 5.8: Exchange Rates and Money Supplies, Nominal Quantities 1971.10–1979.12

Dependent Variable = $\Delta E_t/E_t$

	Constant	$\Delta M_t/M_t$	$\Delta M_{t-1}/M_{t-1}$	$\Delta P_{us,t}/P_{us,t}$	λ_t
Without controlling for exponential trend					
	0.043	-0.315	.516	-1.100	---
	(0.916)	(0.753)	(1.259)	(0.257)	
	$\bar{R}^2 = .15$		$F(6,57) = 2.58$		DW = 1.87
Controlling for exponential trend					
	-0.054	-0.854	0.155	1.159	0.0004
	(1.055)	(2.202)	(0.387)	(0.279)	(3.123)
	$\bar{R}^2 = .29$		$F(8,55) = 4.60$		DW = 1.87

Note: Figures in parentheses are t statistics.

REFERENCES

Bordo, M. and E. Choudhri, 1982, Currency substitution and demand for money: some empirical evidence for Canada, *Journal of Money Credit and Banking* 14 (February), 48-57.

Brittain, B., 1981, International currency substitutions and the apparent instability of velocity in some western European economies and in the United States, *Journal of Money Credit and Banking* 13 (May), 135-155.

Calvo, G., 1984, *Lecciones Del Monetarismo: El Cono Sud.* Banco Central de la Republica Dominicana, forthcoming.

Cuddington, J., 1983, Currency substitutability, capital mobility and money demand, *Journal of International Money and Finance* 2 (August), 111-133.

de Macedo, J.B., 1982, Currency diversification and export competitiveness: a model of the 'Dutch disease' in Egypt, *Journal of Development Economics* (December).

de Macedo, J.B., 1983, Currency inconvertibility, portfolio balance and relative prices, in *Dynamic Modelling and Control of National Economies,* T. Basar and L.F. Pau, eds., 4th IFACS Conference proceedings, 381-385.

Krugman, P., 1980, Vehicle currencies and the structure of international exchange, *Journal of Money Credit and Banking* 12 (August), 513-526.

McKinnon, R., 1982, Currency substitution and instability in the World Dollar Standard, *American Economic Review* (June), 320-333.

Ortiz, G. and L. Solis, 1979, Financial structure and exchange rate experience: Mexico, 1954-1977, *Journal of Development Economics* 6, 515-548.

Sjaastad, L., 1983, Failure of economic liberalism in the core of Latin America, *World Economic Affairs* 1, 5-26.

Vogel, R., 1974, The dynamics of inflation in Latin America, 1950-1969, *American Economic Review* 64 (March), 102-114.

CHAPTER 6

Venezuela and Ecuador —
Currency Substitution in Oil Economies

This chapter continues the empirical investigation of the currency substitution models of Chapters 2 and 3 by approaching the statistical analysis of model predicted phenomena in an indirect way. In the previous chapters we examined descriptively the impact of qualitative policy changes and statistically the shape of the money demand function for the Dominican Republic, a small open economy. We also examined the effect of liberalization by estimating money demand functions across regime changes for Argentina, a large, sometimes open economy. In this chapter we will compare two economies who had somewhat similar exogenous experiences to learn more about how policy induced changes in money demand engender phenomena similar to those predicted by our model. Specifically, we will be looking at the time series properties of money and prices in Venezuela and in Ecuador, two oil dependent economies, over the period 1970 to 1983.

We employ the indirect method of drawing inferences because it permits us to make use of frequently observed measures, and hence more data points, and because we are able to employ data with which we have some confidence. In the direct analyses of the previous chapters the specification of the model and the implemented statistical analyses were perforce predicated on certain unmeasured statistical relationships being held constant. We now weaken that assumption at the expense of not being able to estimate directly our economic model. Rather we will describe and draw inferences about the theory from a careful examination of the statistical properties of the data.

The two economies we are studying, Venezuela and Ecuador are best described as oil-growth economies. The existence of petroleum reserves was well known in both countries in 1970, and exploration of these reserves was well under way. The impact of the oil price shock of 1973 was dramatic in both cases. Both countries began receiving massively increased revenues from the their production of petroleum. Both countries employed these newly acquired riches to finance development plans and to fuel economic growth. Moreover, although both invested heavily in infrastructure and created the basis for expanded economic activity in other sectors, at the end of our study period, petroleum revenues remained the single most imporant generator of foreign exchange and remained one of the key elements of public finance. The case of petroleum countries is particularly interesting for our study as the exportation of petroleum generates huge dollar earnings and lowers the cost of using dollars in two ways. First the ready availability of dollars implies that physical use costs are lower. Second, the close connection between domestic economic activity and the dollar value of petroluem, all petroleum export contracts being written in dollars, means that the marginal costs of obtaining sufficient information to use dollars in transactions is lower. With all of these factors in common, we will attribute differences in the way in which prices respond to changes in the quantity of money with differences in government policies.

1. STABILITY AND HOMOGENEITY

The years between 1970 and 1983 were important in the evolution of the Venezuelan and Ecuadorian economies. During this time it was realized that neither need follow the traditional routes to rapid economic growth in order to develop; that of a large infusions of foreign capital coupled with high domestic savings rates and socially disruptive reallocations of domestic resources. Rather, each come to the opinion that governments share of petrodollars, earnings from the export of petroleum, could be used to finance ambitious growth plans. In 1973 the OPEC nations, of which

Venezuela and Ecuador are two, collectively increased the price
of oil fourfold. This generated large surpluses and an ability to
modernize without pain. Since oil prices are quoted in dollars, the
real value of these earnings decreased through the decade of the
70's. Thus by the latter part of the decade the purchasing power
of saved petrodollars and newly gained export earnings impinged
on development planning. Moreover, the previous growth in development projects was hindered by a lack of growth in export
earnings. A brief reprieve came in 1979 with the second large oil
price shock however its benefits were short lived.

The two countries we are considering made considerable pro-
gress towards generating modern economic structures during this
time. While Venezuela has a much larger pool of petroleum reserves than Ecuador, the impact of the shock on the two countries
was at first glance approximately the same. This was probably
because Ecuador at the beginning of the decade was much poorer
than Venezuela and therefore the percentage of per capita GNP
represented by the new oil earnings was approximately the same.
In Venezuela the petrodollars were funnelled into the Fondo de
Inversiones de Venezuela (Venezuelan Investment Fund) to be dis-
persed for development projects. In Ecuador the new oil revenues
were used to support the development plan of CONADE, the na-

tional planning ministry. As is to be expected, many parts of the government and non-government sectors of the economy placed claims on the new wealth, but the basic purpose to which it was put and which is central to our analysis, was to support economic growth and development.

The history of money and prices can be illustrated by a brief glance at Table 6.1. In the first three years of the decade inflation rates were relatively low. The higher growth rates of the money stock in both countries was therefore used to support growing market transactions and were therefore non-inflationary. The rapid growth after 1973 is indicated by the very high money growth rates in each country through the end of the decade. In Venezuela the money stock grew at an average rate of 30.3 per cent between 1973 and 1978 while inflation was only at an annual average of 7.9 per cent. In Ecuador money growth was an average 26.7 for the same period and inflation 15.4 per cent. The higher inflation rate for Ecuador indicates the government was more excessive than Venezuela in providing a monetary background for growth. Nevertheless the rates of inflation were not out of line with world rates of inflation and were certainly below those experienced by many neighboring countries. From 1979 to 1983, in spite of the new oil price hike, rates of inflation in both countries were approximately

Table 6.1: Money Emission and Price Inflation

	Venezuela		Ecuador	
	Growth of M1	Inflation	Growth of M1	Inflation
1970	7.3	3.3	23.9	8.3
1971	19.6	2.7	13.7	14.0
1972	12.2	3.3	21.6	6.9
1973	23.0	5.3	31.9	20.6
1974	40.8	11.6	37.7	23.6
1975	53.9	8.0	16.1	11.4
1976	17.1	7.0	38.1	13.1
1977	26.0	8.1	22.2	12.9
1978	21.0	7.1	14.1	10.8
1979	6.7	20.5	17.0	10.0
1980	13.7	19.6	20.0	13.5
1981	7.1	11.0	11.3	15.6
1982	-8.2	7.3	20.7	24.9

Note: M1 figures are end of month totals. Prices are urban CPI indexes. Sources: Bulletins of the Banco Central de Venezuela and Banco Central de Ecuador.

equal to or greater than the rates of money growth. This possibly indicates a change in policy or a reaction to current policy on the part of the population. These apparent changes will be examined below.

We begin our more careful analysis by transforming the original unadjusted money and price series to be stationary time series. First, each series was transformed by taking logarithms. This transformation linearizes most standard money demand equations and is therefore appropriate for our econometric analysis. All four series were examined for the presence of trend components by regression analysis. That is, the levels of the series were projected on a trend variable, t, and a significant relation was found. We removed this deterministic component and conducted the remainder of our analysis on deviation from trend time series. The removal of trends are controversial since an apparent deterministic trend may be an artifact of a random walk filter applied to a white noise stochastic process. To be sure that our methodology is not inducing spurious time series correlations by assuming to be deterministic what is in fact random, we conducted our analysis a second time on differenced rather than detrended data. The substantive inferential results remained unchanged with differenced data and we therefore present only the detrended results. In addition we filtered our time series for seasonal components but found very little seasonality in the data.

Our interest is the bivariate stochastic process $\big(P_i(t), M_i(t)\big)$ where the index i denotes the country, and P, the price level, and M, the money stock, are detrended. To examine the stability of the money to price relation we estimated the following equation:

$$P_i(t) = \sum_{j=1}^{4} \beta_j P_i(t-j) + \sum_{j=5}^{8} \beta_j M_i(t-j) D_i(t-j)$$

$$+ \sum_{j=9}^{12} \beta_j M_i(t-j)\big(1 - D_i(t-j)\big) + U_i(t) \quad (6.1.1)$$

Equation (6.1.1) is a reduced form equation consistent with many different theories of the relation between money and prices. For a rational expectations model such as those of Sargent and Wallace (1973), current prices depend on future values of the money stock. In a stationary environment this may be well represented by a distributed lag on past money stocks as in (6.1.1). For partial adjustment or adaptive expectations models a distributed lag such as (6.1.1) is also appropriate. In addition, theories of inertial price inflation are consistent with this reduced form. To go beyond (6.1.1) to infer the nature of price inflation in Venezuela and Ecuador by eliminating coefficients in structural models requires identification criteria or assumptions. We choose to avoid this problem as our interest is not in testing alternative theories with our inadequate data but in providing indirect evidence on time series properties.

We define the variable D_i as a country specific dummy variable for purposes of testing hypotheses about the stability of coefficients.

$$D_i(t) = \begin{cases} 0 & t \leq \ell \\ 1 & t > \ell \end{cases} \tag{6.1.2}$$

Since we do not know exactly when a break in these series might occur, we examine the time series by letting ℓ vary from June 1975 to December 1978. In this way any major change in the relation between M and P will be captured by our tests and we can evaluate the test results for the appropriate break point. Identifying breaks in series with particular policy changes is a somewhat subtle exercise as is indicated by our economic theory. This is because behavior ought to change in response to the knowledge that policy will change as well as to the policy change itself. Thus we find it more fruitful to take a data based approach here.

To examine stability of coefficients we test the joint hypothesis $\beta_5 = \beta_9$, $\beta_6 = \beta_{10}$, $\beta_7 = \beta_{11}$ and $\beta_8 = \beta_{12}$ for each of the candidate break points from 1975 to 1978. For each a restricted and unrestricted model was estimated. Define N as the number of observations, Σ_1 as the sum of squared residuals from the restricted model and Σ_2 as that from the unrestricted model; then the statistic $T(\ell n \; \Sigma_1 - \ell n \; \Sigma_2)$ is asymptotically distributed χ^2 with the number of degrees of freedom equal to the number of restrictions, under the null hypothesis that the restrictions are valid. Tables 6.2 and 6.3 present the results of our stability tests for Venezuela and Ecuador respectively. The lag lengths of our vector autoregresions were examined and we settled on four lags for the Venezuelan model and six for the Ecuadorian model. In addition a dummy variable was introduced for the 1979-1980 liberalization of price setting in commodity markets in Venezuela to pick up a mean shift, if one existed.

For Venezuela we find marginal significance levels of less that 5% in 1975, but none thereafter. Indeed the hypothesis of changing coefficients before and after 1975 was strongly rejected. This suggests that the instability we find in the coefficients was in the earliest part of our sample. Recall that prior to 1973, petroleum, while important in Venezuela, did not have the same influence as after October 1973. We suspect that the evidence for Venezuela reflects the temporary disruption of the 1973 OPEC oil price rise and not a fundamental change in the money to price pattern. Leaving the first couple of years out of our sample confirms this and we therefore infer that the time series are characterized best as a

Table 6.2: Test of Stability of Coefficients Between
          Prices and Money: Venezuela 1970-1983

Sample Break After	$\chi^2(4)$	Marginal Significance Level
75,6	10.00	.04
75,12	10.63	.03
76,6	6.46	.17
76,12	3.21	.52
77,6	2.56	.63
77,12	1.03	.91
78,6	1.61	.81
78,12	1.87	.76

Data: Bulletin of Banco Central de Venezuela.

Table 6.3: Tests of Stability of Coefficients Between
          Prices and Money: Ecuador 1969-1982

Sample Break After	$\chi^2(6)$	Marginal Significance Level
75,6	8.42	.21
75,12	8.39	.21
76,6	8.40	.21
76,12	9.18	.16
77,6	14.67	.02
77,12	18.64	.01
78,6	31.33	.00
78,12	31.08	.00

Data: Bulletin of Banco Central de Ecuador.

single bivariate process during the ten years 1973 to 1983.

For Ecuador the results are surprisingly different. We employed a six lag structure for Ecuador because it yielded a better fit to the data and tested jointly the stability of the six coefficients on lagged money stocks. Our results for the four lag model were not substantially different. Overall we find marginal significance levels considerably lower than Venezuela and the pattern is quite different. For sample break points after January 1977 the data strongly reject stability of money stock coefficients. The marginal significance levels are at most 2%. Since the broad economic history of the two countries is the same, such a different pattern in coefficient stability must be attributable to different policies.

One obvious difference between the two countries was that foreign exchange markets were more open in Ecuador than in Venezuela. While the period of the 1970's showed a great deal of stability in the fixed exchange rate of Venezuela and the floating rate of Ecuador, toward the end of the 1970's and early 1980's exchange rate pressure in Venezuela resulted in some small devaluations and controls. In Ecuador the result was a rapid depreciation of the international value of the currency. By the end of 1982 the value of the Ecuadorian sucre was one-third its mid 1970's value. However before we draw strong conclusions from this one statistical test we wish to explore more deeply the seemingly different patterns from the two countries.

The next part of our specification analysis is to test the exogeneity of money in the money-price model. This is an important specification test as a change in the money growth rule from passive to active may well reflect merely policy changes but may distort our statistical analysis. Table 6.4 presents our test results for the two countries. The test we employ comes from estimating the first equation from the VAR and appending leads to the right hand side. We then test the restriction that these leads have coefficients not significantly different from zero. For Venezuela we find that the hypothesis that money is exogenous to prices is valid at a very high significance level. For Ecuador we estimated the model with 6 leads because of a lack of data in one subsample. Our estimates yield F statistic values for the entire sample and for the period up to 1977 which are sufficiently small to conclude that money is exogenous. For the period 1977 to 1982 the marginal significance level falls to 6%. This means that at a 5% level we can still conclude that money is exogenous, and we are more confident with the inference because the small number of denominator degrees of freedom for the F statistic. However, we ought to be cautious about this interpretation.

Table 6.4: Exogeneity Tests on Money Stocks:
          Venezuela and Ecuador 1970-1983

1970-1983 Venezuela: Null Hypothesis; coefficients on
                      future values of M are zero.

  $F(8,139) = 0.72$ Marginal Significance = .67

1969-1982 Ecuador

  $F(6,137) = 0.30$ Marginal Significance = .94

1969-1977 Ecuador

  $F(6,77) = 0.76$ Marginal Significance = .60

1979-1982 Ecuador

  $F(6,17) = 2.56$ Marginal Significance = .06

In Tables 6.5 and 6.6 we present our estimated distributed lag
models. The estimated coefficients are from the same regression
as the Sims exogeneity test regression. In each case the coefficients
are not very revealing by themselves. However jointly they explain
much of the variation in prices. This is probably a result of past
prices containing much information about future prices, a condition documented for U.S. prices during the 1970's by Nickelsburg
(1982). This phenomena appears to occur when in the absence of
real price shocks, of which there were many in the 1970's, there
would have been relatively stable prices. However, this hypothesis

Table 6.5: Price Equation — Ecuador

Variable	Lag	Coefficient	Standard Error	Marginal Significance
		1969-1977		
Price	1	.76	.11	.00
	2	.06	.14	.69
	3	-.16	.14	.26
	4	.14	.14	.33
	5	.13	.14	.36
	6	-.16	.11	.16
Money	1	.0003	.0076	.96
	2	-.0030	.0075	.68
	3	-.0049	.0075	.51
	4	-.0007	.0075	.92
	5	-.0003	.0074	.96
	6	.0003	.0075	.96

$R^2 = .66$ DW = 2.03   Degrees of freedom = 77

Variable	Lag	Coefficient	Standard Error	Marginal Significance
		1979-1982		
Price	1	.47	.22	.05
	2	-.12	.24	.64
	3	-.005	.24	.99
	4	.30	.25	.24
	5	-.15	.26	.57
	6	.09	.18	.61
Money	1	-1.08	2.31	.65
	2	.39	2.42	.87
	3	.85	2.47	.74
	4	-.56	2.43	.82
	5	.85	2.40	.73
	6	4.07	2.12	.07

$R^2 = .92$ DW = 2.11   Degrees of freedom = 17

Table 6.6: Price Equation — Venezuela, 1970-1983

Variable	Lag	Coefficient	Standard Error	Marginal Significance
Price	1	1.27	.08	.00
	2	-0.12	.14	.36
	3	-0.07	.14	.59
	4	-0.10	.08	.22
Money	1	-0.45	.03	.15
	2	-0.01	.03	.59
	3	-0.04	.03	.20
	4	-0.02	.02	.36

$R^2 = .99$ DW = 2.02   Degrees of freedom = 139

is conjecture at this point.

We conclude this section by noting that we have observed two different basic money price histories and attribute them to different exchange rate policies. But, the exchange rate itself is merely an outlet for internal economic pressure. We believe that the key element can be found in the development plans of the two countries. In Ecuador, the increase in oil revenues generated a very quick response in development plans. Thus, the government swung into action with new infrastructure programs and consumed the new revenue. By the mid 1970's the growth in oil revenues had

flattened out and was declining in real terms. In order to maintain the growth in development programs the Ecuadorian government resorted to foreign borrowing and increased money creation.
These two actions are inconsistent with long run price stability unless they are viewed by the public as simply temporary measures.
Consequently in Ecuador a capital flight began in the late 1970's
to avoid the incipient inflation tax, and the velocity of money increased. Each increase in the quantity of money then generated
new flights of liquid capital and exchange rate depreciation —
events we pick up in our analysis.

In Venezuela the impact of the oil price shock was not immediate in its full measure. Election campaigns and uncertainty about
the direction of new development plans engendered a diversion of
large parts of the new oil wealth into the Fondo de Inversiones
de Venezuela. These accumulated resources permitted Venezuela
to avoid the slowdown in development programs in the late 70's
as they were available to make up for declining real oil revenues.
Thus, the experience of Ecuador in the early 1970's was stretched
out over the decade in Venezuela. In 1983, when the FIV resources
were badly depleted the currency crisis-capital flight experience of
Ecuador was repeated in Venezuela.

Our evidence thus far is indirect and indicates two separate episodes of monetary phenomena for Ecuador and one for Venezuela. These could be because of disparate fiscal policies with and without currency substitution. The role played by foreign currencies here could only be the following. In Ecuador dollars were readily available in the open market. Thus it would have been easy to substitute away from the domestic currency. In Venezuela dollars were available, but because of currency restriction they were more costly. The crises of Latin American countries in the late 70's and the running down of the FIV funds should have given Venezuelans ample incentive to leave the domestic currency. That they did not indicates either confidence in their government to not employ the inflation tax or that the marginal cost of using dollars was higher. The information costs of using dollars in the two economies should have been the same as they were both oil economies and therefore the cost differential must be due to currency restrictions.

2. FREQUENCY ANALYSIS OF MONEY AND PRICES

Whenever we analyze the relation between money and prices there is always a concern that short-run price responses to changes in the quantity of money may mask a fundamental long run effect. The idea of the neutrality of money, that doubling the money stock will double all prices is a powerful idea in economic theory, and with good reason. Any violation of this principle must come about through dynamic processes and any market imperfection will result in non-neutral, but temporary, changes in prices. To get at this issue we decompose our series on money and prices into their respective frequency components. We then examine the strength of coherence between money and prices at alternative frequencies and the degree to which frequency components are out of phase.

Our methodology of analysis is to take the fast Fourier transform of each money and price time series and compute the spectrum for the money stock and the CPI and the co-spectra of the two. These are presented in Table 6.7. For Ecuador we estimated the spectra for the two subperiods found in the last section with a break in the series at 1977. The co-spectra which appear in the tables are broken into coherence and phase components. The spectra were each constructed with a Parzan window of width 5. For details on the construction of confidence intervals see Fuller (1976), pp. 308-326.

An examination of Table 6.7 reveals that the early Ecuador period, 1970-1977 looks very much like the entire Venezuela episode. For Ecuador there is a short-run impact of money on prices

Table 6.7: Coherence and Phase Spectra

| | Ecuador | | | | Venezuela | |
| | 1969-1977 | | 1978-1982 | | 1970-1982 | |
Period	Co.	Phase	Co.	Phase	Co.	Phase
2	.72*	-0.43*	.76*	.73*	.64	0.04
3	.35	-0.51	.78*	-.67*	.90*	-.78*
4	.19	-1.68	.89*	1.42*	.48	0.33
5	.28	-1.28	.59*	1.62*	.23	1.03
6	.23	0.58	.66*	.33	.79*	-.45**
12	.35	1.44	.95*	5.80*	.54	-.29
24	.34	-3.48	.70*	-7.24*	.38	5.33
36	.41	11.09	.25	-3.06*	.79*	5.24*

*Significant at the 5% level.
**Significant at the 10% level.

with periodicity of two months and a slight phase shift towards money leading prices. This is perhaps anticipatory or coincident price increases since our data are end of month figures for the money stock. The remaining frequencies reveal no relation between money and prices. It should be noted that the phase shift is significant only when it is sufficiently different from zero and the coherence is significantly different from zero. In the early Ecuador period only one coherence estimate was significant and therefore only one phase shift hypothesis test of significance was performed.

For Venezuela over the entire period there are three significant coherence estimates. First, the periodicity 3 coherence is significant and the phase shift, also significant, indicates that prices lead money somewhat. These estimates are for a very short run component and may be considered once again impact effects. The only other significant component is a six month effect. While this is still short-run, it is more difficult to make the case that this is an impact effect. However, there are many prices for "basic needs" goods which are controlled, and we suspect that the timing of these price changes reflects a process of semi-annual review of prices. This could explain both the six month coherence and the weak evidence of a price leading money phase shift. The phase shift has a marginal significance level between 5 and 10% and may be considered insignificant for some tests. The longer run relation between money and prices reveals three year effect. There is a high coherence between money and prices, and money strongly leads prices. This is consistent with our previous results, but differs somewhat from the early Ecuador results. In Nickelsburg (1986) this same long run effect was found for Ecuador prior to 1973. In both cases we find the money stock having the usually predicted impact on the level of prices.

For the second Ecuador period, 1977-1982, we find a large

number of significant coherence estimates. In the short-run, all of
the estimates for periodicity of six months or less are significant.
Moreover their phase shifts are significant and except for three
months peridocity, reflect money leading prices. Thus the impact
and short-run processes in the late Ecuador period is a change in
the quantity of money causing a change in the price level in the
same direction. However, for the two and three year periodic components we have a different and more anomolous result. Namely,
the lead of money over prices is reversed. We must discount the
three year coherence estimate because it is not significant but there
is a strong two year phase shift. Since the periodicity is so long, it
is difficult to attribute prices leading money in the late Ecuador period to anticipations. Rather it must be that prices have become,
in their long run components, exogenous and monetary policy is
accommodating this.

3. CONCLUDING REMARKS

To summarize our results from this chapter we have found
that the basic patterns of money and prices for Ecuador and
Venezuela were the same over the seven year period from 1970
to 1977. The pattern in Venezuela seems to have persisted into
the early 1980's while in Ecuador the pattern changed in the late

1970's. Our explanation for this is two-fold. First the key difference in monetary regimes was that Ecuador permitted free substitution of foreign currency. Second, the economic development activity on the part of the government relied on oil revenues for both countries with Venezuela spreading out their windfall gains over a decade and a half and Ecuador spreading them over only about five years. Thus Ecuador was forced to employ monetary policy to continue the momentum begun by the infusion of oil profits.

These two policy differences permitted Ecuadorians to avoid the inflation tax of government deficits by going into other currencies and foreign sources of wealth. The impetus for this was not felt in the early Ecuador period as the government could engage in more conservative monetary policies while exploiting their newly acquired wealth. Thus we have provided evidence that access to dollars with readily accessible information about their value will result in rapid capital flight and substitution away from the domestic currency.

REFERENCES

Fuller, Wayne A., 1976, *Introduction to Statistical Time Series*, John Wiley & Sons: New York, 308-326.

Marquez, J., 1985, Money demand in open economies: a currency substitution model for Ecuador, manuscript, International Division, Federal Reserve Board.

Marquez, J., 1986, Inflation and relative prices: an empirical note on the Venezuelan experience, manuscript, International Division, Federal Reserve Board.

McNelis, Paul and Gerald Nickelsburg, 1986, Money, prices and dollarization: evidence from Peru and Ecuador, mimeo.

Nickelsburg, Gerald, 1982, Foreign exchange rate theories: the time series evidence, *Time Series Theory and Practice* 2, O.D. Anderson, ed., 61-74.

Nickelsburg, Gerald, forthcoming 1986, Inflation expectations and qualitative government policy, *World Development*.

Sargent, Thomas J. and Neil Wallace, 1973, The stability of models of money and growth with perfect foresight, *Econometrica* 41, 1043-1048.

Sims, Christopher A., 1972, Money incomes and causality, *The American Economic Review* 62, 540-552.

CHAPTER 7

Conclusion

In this volume we have examined the phenomenon of currency substitution from many different angles. Our examination posed the questions, can such a phenomenon have a theoretical basis for its existence, and if so is it an important phenomenon? In Chapters 2 and 3 we provided answers in the affirmative to these questions. The models we analyzed were somewhat specialized, but suggested a line of research which maybe richly rewarding. The overlapping generations framework of Chapter 2 permitted us to focus on some specific aspects of monetary choice in a consistent and complete way. The framework is limited since it becomes intractably complicated for richer models. For example the introduction of heterogeneity and the comparative advantage basis for trade are important extensions to the basic framework not undertaken here. The model of Chapter 3, while suggested by the model of Chapter 2, does not have a firm basis in optimizing behavior. However it did permit us to characterize in a more general way the effects of policy on equilibria and its implications for the relationship between time series observations. Thus, while we have constructed internally consistent theories at microfoundation and at macro levels to support the idea of currency substitution equilibrium, much has yet to be done.

In the second part of this volume we analyzed in three different ways the experiences of Latin America in light of our theory. The countries we analyzed were chosen because of the variety they present. The Dominican Republic was the smallest of these and clearly satisfies the small open economy assumptions. Our model should work for a country which is large, but which because of past policies has a currency which is dominated by another readily available currency. Such a country is Argentina and we found that indeed the monetary history of Argentina was completely consistent with our theoretical constructs. Finally we examined two resource wealthy countries, Venezuela and Ecuador to see if liberal international monetary policies, practically the only way in which they differed during the 1970's would lead to different monetary phenomena. One theory suggests that Ecuador with its open exchange markets would be less able to influence prices with monetary policy than would Venezuela. Our empirical analysis confirms this. These results suggest that if one were to impose a stabilization policy to reduce the rate of inflation, the appropriate monetary arrangements would involve closing off access to foreign money except by prior governmental approval.

The major difficulty we encountered while trying to empirically analyze the phenomenon of currency substitution was the lack of a direct test of the theory. This is because the theory displays its unique character in general equilibrium models and these are very hard to test. In less demanding models there exist too many alternative interpretations of the data. One is therefore faced to test the theory by providing evidence indirectly. Perhaps an analysis of deeper microeconomic data is warranted to further this area.

In conclusion we have found that government policy in open economies can lead to currency flight and the substitution of foreign money for domestic money. This phenomenon is merely the choice by individuals to avoid an inflation tax and has two basic implications. First, countries are constrained internationally in the kinds of policies they can reasonably follow over the long-run. Second, if a country which has the preconditions for capital flight or currency substitution wishes to pursue a policy of deficit financing through inflation, it must be willing to intervene in the foreign exchange market to control the use of the foreign currency. This can be accomplished by increasing the cost of using the foreign currency. In our theory we gave examples of threatened interventions, taxation of currency flows and taxation of currency stocks. Also, if policy maintains an exchange rate which depreciates at the rate of domestic inflation over foreign inflation, we have shown it can be an optimal inflation financing program. Finally our results suggests that developing country monetary theory and policy might be properly viewed as different in kind from developed country monetary theory and policy. This distinction may well help explain other apparently anomalous macroeconomic phenomena.

INDEX

ABOUT THE AUTHORS

Dr. Victor A. Canto received a B.Sc. from M.I.T. and an M.A. and Ph.D. in Economics from the University of Chicago. He is currently Senior Vice President and Director of Research at A.B. Laffer Associates. He has been an Assistant Professor and an Associate Professor at the University of Southern California as well as Visiting Professor at the Universidad Central Del Este, Dominican Republic.

Dr. Canto has also served as economics advisor to the Finance Minister of the Dominican Republic, economist for the economics studies division of the Dominican Republic Central Bank, as well as a consultant to Puerto Rico's Treasury and Government Financial Council.

His other books include *Foundations of Supply Side Economics, Apuntaciones Sobre Inflación y Politica Economica en Republica Dominicana, The Financial Analyst's Guide to Monetary Policy, The Financial Analyst's Guide to Fiscal Policy, The Determinant and Consequences of Trade Restrictions in the U.S.*

Economy, and *Industrial Policy and International Trade.* His publications have appeared in the *Economic Inquiry, Southern Economic Journal, Public Finance, Journal of International Money and Finance, The International Trade Journal* and the *Journal of Macroeconomics,* among others.

Dr. Gerald Nickelsburg received a B.A. from the George Washington University, and M.A. from the University of Colorado and a Ph.D. from the University of Minnesota. He is currently an Assistant Professor of Economics at the University of Southern California. He has also been a Fulbright Scholar in Ecuador, a consultant to the Ministry of Commerce in Peru, and a staff member of the Federal Reserve Board.

Dr. Nickelsburg has published articles on monetary economics, econometrics and international economics in the *Review of Economic Studies, Journal of Development Economics, Journal of Econometrics* and *Journal of Monetary Economics* among others.